The Craft of Comedy Writing

SOL SAKS

Cincinnati, Ohio

Library of Congress Cataloging in Publication Data

Saks, Sol, 1910-
   The craft of comedy writing.

   Includes index.
   1. Wit and humor—Authorship. 2. Comedy—Authorship.
I. Title.
PN6149.A88S24   1985   808.7   85-14386
ISBN 0-89879-192-8

Design by Alice Mauro

Contents

Introduction

There is humor in every aspect of our lives and environments. We use it to make friends, to turn away anger, to cover inadequacies, to earn a living, to get laid, to gain revenge, to sell beer, to spread sunshine, to endure the intolerable, to cover embarrassment, to hurt and to heal.

It is offered as a gift, a blow, or a product for sale.

This book endeavors to treat its more pragmatic forms, for those of us who do it primarily for a livelihood and for those who use it as a tool in other fields.

Comedy is an important element in every art form; including music, dance, art, and mime. However, since this book is by a writer for writers, we will deal only in those fields which need and are willing to pay for our services.

The arenas are television, the cinema, the stage, night clubs, the after-dinner speech, articles, books, cartoons, comic strips, advertising, and greeting cards.

Since today the largest, most active and usually best paying markets for humor are in the theatrical, motion picture, and television fields—and coincidentally, these are the areas of my major experience—the emphasis of this book will be on script comedy.

I had intended this book to be objective. To my dismay, it is not only subjective in parts but, occasionally autobiographical. I don't like using myself in examples, but I have no other choices or volunteers.

My first ambitions as a writer were to write erudite essays and slice-of-life short stories that would appear in obscure literary magazines. I still nurture and sometimes try to gratify that ambition. The trouble was that my second most important goal was to earn a living. So when I found that everyone with a type-writer—or sometimes only a brown piece of paper and a pencil—was my competitor, and that at the word comedy, four-fifths of the competition faded away, that was where I set up my lemonade stand.

In those days, radio comedy writing was the most accessible opening to a writing career, and the only immediate escape if I was to stay out of the family business. And radio comedy was jokes. So . . . I learned to write jokes.

Writing jokes is an acquired skill. As a youngster, I not only wasn't the funniest kid on the block, I wasn't even the funniest one among my two buddies. My two friends—who both said funnier things than I did—were amazed when I was the one who made a career of it. There was a simple explanation. I had the motivation. I don't know exactly what talent is, but I suspect that it's often a synonym for motivation.

The famous and beautiful don't have to be funny, except for their own amusement. We others need to be, if we want to be invited back.

I remember my first, frightening steps into comedy writing—a desperate, random groping for something funny. A feeling similar to the actor's nightmare of being on stage in an unknown play of which he doesn't remember the lines.

A major purpose of this book is that others may avoid some of the painful blundering most of us went through.

Comedy writing is not an exact science. It's not like learning to fly a 747. It's more difficult, takes quite a bit longer, and is more dangerous. In this book I've tried to teach that which is teachable, explain what is explainable, and demonstrate what is demonstrable.

We will discuss the principles of comedy, the raw materials of comedy, the construction of comedy, the varieties of comedy, the uses of comedy, the problems of comedy, the rewards of comedy and, to the best of my ability, the marketing of comedy. We'll identify the principles and characteristics that apply to all forms of humor writing.

I've tried to put in everything I know about comedy writing. I'm afraid, in my eagerness, I may have included some I don't know. I did my best to indicate which was opinion, which was conjecture, and what I knew for sure. Perhaps I should have restricted myself to the latter, but that would have made this a very thin book.

·1·

Operator's Manual
for the
Comedy Writer

*"Just take a piece of ivory
and cut away everything
that isn't walrus."*

First off, you should know that this is a book by a writer who doesn't believe in textbooks, about a subject he believes is unteachable. At this point you have the option to return the book, or at least exchange it for one on how to make love—which is also unteachable but at least that book will have interesting illustrations. There are four modern curses that I believe arrived disguised as blessings: polyester, aerosol cans, copying machines, and how-to books. But here I go.

Be warned that this book is opinionated, usually undocumented and nonscientific. Humor may be a science, but when treated as such it's incomprehensible and unrewarding.

First, a few unadorned truths. Anybody can write. On the other hand, anybody can be a stripper, too—but unless you've got the equipment *and* the motivation, you probably shouldn't try to do either for a living.

Be prepared to fall on your ass. If you don't fall on your ass every once in awhile, you're not really trying. Your writing, like almost anything else in life, is never as bad as you feared—or as good as you dreamed.

Follow your instincts. If your instincts conflict with logic, forget the logic. Instincts are incorruptible, but logic often betrays you.

Which leads us to the next admonition—be bold. Take chances. An integral part of comedy is surprise, which means it's new, which means you're not sure if it's going to work.

There are no rules for writing, only techniques. Techniques, or rules if you insist, are simply methods that past practitioners have found efficacious. They were not brought down by Moses from Mount Sinai. (As a matter of fact, I can think of at least one of the original ones that could use revision.) It is helpful to learn these techniques, but once you have learned them, you are at liberty to ignore them, change them, or best of all, make up your own. The final criterion is telling a story well and if you can do that by having your characters hanging upside down (Beckett had them sitting in a garbage can)—do it, for Godsake, do it. Many, perhaps most, of the best things in the world are done by people breaking rules. Technique all by itself is what makes for hack writers.

Anybody can communicate anything if he keeps writing long enough. It is said that if a million apes were to pound on a million typewriters for a million years, they would eventually write *Hamlet*. Isn't it fortunate for us that a man named William Shakespeare saved us not only all those years, repairing all those typewriters, and feeding all those apes, but the chore of going through mountains of pages to find it.

Freud and Darwin were both preceded in their discoveries, but they communicated them better. America was named after the man who wrote about it, not the man who discovered it.

In Alaska anthropologists once found a tiny, beautifully sculptured figure of a walrus carved by an Eskimo. When they asked him how he did it, he replied, "I just took a piece of ivory and cut away everything that wasn't walrus." That's what this book is all about. Cutting away everything that isn't walrus.

Modern man walks a very narrow ridge between boredom and hysteria. It's the artist's function to help him maintain his balance. The humorist's function is to help him forget his fear. Man is the only one of God's creatures who feels guilt and is aware of his own mortality; he is also the only one who can laugh, an accomplishment probably given to him so that he can deal with the first two.

We are all of us crazy in some way or other. Fortunately for our civilization, most of us are crazy in socially acceptable ways. Successful humor is that which appeals to those tolerable insanities.

Mark Twain said that we shouldn't require a humorist to paint himself striped and stand on his head. But to start with, a humorist must be one who knows we are all some kind of fool and is willing to admit it, who has a compulsive preference for the short odds, and has decided to use humor to protect himself from the slings and arrows of outrageous fortune. One who has the unselfconsciousness of a child and uses the God-given right to make a spectacle of himself.

On the other hand we are fortunate, as actors, dancers, singers, musicians, and all other artists are fortunate, in that we never had to put aside our childish things. The clown hides behind a painted face, the comic in baggy pants, the jester in a fool's cap, but the writer won't come out on the stage at all. He slips the words under the door, listens to them read through a keyhole, and cries silently when they are misquoted.

To write comedy—or any other form for that matter—requires a combination of arrogance and humility. The need for arrogance is obvious; to believe that you can hold the attention of strangers—much less make them laugh—shows a self-confidence that defies logic. Humility is essential if you are ever going to improve, to realize how easy it is to fail, and more important, to accept that people who may wear wing-tip shoes, drink soda pop with steak, and answer quizzes in magazines to find out if they're good lovers, will—and should be—the final, undisputed judges on whether you are bringing it off.

One of the important functions of humor is to get people to *listen*. That's why the after-dinner speaker likes to start with "A funny thing happened on my way over here tonight. . . ." And just watch those apathetic people, stuffed with fried chicken and mashed potatoes, perk up.

That's why it's used to sell something, illustrate dull instructions, or win your vote. To hold your attention. The President of the United States usually has a joke writer on his staff to make unpopular announcements palatable. (It might be a commentary on our civilization that ancient rulers had jesters to make themselves happy, and today jesters are used to make the subjects happy—which seems like a step in the right direction.)

People who won't stop for an attractive model, or a beautiful picture, or a strident command, will stop for a laugh. Before you can get people to pay attention, or follow instructions, or hear your side of it, or buy something, you've got to get them to *listen*. So be sure a funny thing happens on your way over. . . .

Comedy must be economical, or as it was said much better in the above-mentioned play by the million apes, "Brevity is the soul of wit."

In a paper on humor, Freud quotes a V. Fischer as saying, "Wit is a playful judgment." Humor is defined as a perception of the incongruous. So there you have it in a nutshell—a perception of the incongruous, a playful judgment and get off.

Let's put it another way.

Pick a good story, tell it well, and get it out into the marketplace. That's all there is to it. That's what this book is about.

·2·

What's Funny?

*There is no such thing
as the quite successful comedian,
just as there is no such thing
as the quite successful God.*
SYDNEY COX

What's funny?

Anything and everything. That is, if that's the way you see it. Comedy is not a counterpart of drama, it is a subdivision. It is simply the mood and attitude you have decided on to tell your story.

And what is that mood? It is the tilted look, the unorthodox angle, the unexpected point of view, the outrageous comment, the irreverent posture, and above all, thinking as well as feeling. If we can put misfortune in the proper perspective, we can use humor to show the foolishness of our anxieties, the absurdity of our anger, and we make the unbearable bearable. (Horace Walpole once said, "The world is a comedy to those that think, a tragedy to those that feel.")

The attitude and mood of comedy is the decision to disavow the heat and pain of living. We use it because we're too big to cry but not mature enough to dismiss it.

Example: There's nothing inherently funny about a beautiful day, a good meal, and a lovely girl—unless it rains, you have no money to pay the check, and the waiter steals your girl. That still isn't comedy but we're getting closer. Now you've got the materials of conflict and misfortune to work with. You've got to get more tragic before you get to funny. Now you step back, look at it from the vantage point of another place, another time, other eyes, and get it into the only perspective that can make it tolerable in this unmanageable, unpredictable world of ours. That's the attitude that makes for comedy.

There have been successful comedies about death, terminal illness, infidelity, physical handicaps, ugliness—because the writer saw them that way. Anything is funny if that's your way of telling a story. One word of caution: if it isn't your way, don't mess with it.

At one time, there were two hit plays running simultaneously on Broadway, *Mr. Roberts* and *The Caine Mutiny*. Both had almost identical basic themes: a dominating, implacable, emotionally retarded sea captain in the United States Navy during wartime. One was a comedy, the other a drama. A further irony is that in the drama, the hero triumphs; in the comedy, he dies.

"Laughing and trembling are so curiously intermingled," Saul Bellow says about ethnic writing, "that it is not easy to determine the relation of the two." Mel Brooks uses another example. "If I cut my finger," he says, "that's a tragedy. If you fall down a sewer, that's comedy."

Some psychiatrists say that all humor is hostile. I tend to suspect psychiatrists of overdramatizing the human state. So, as a writer, I would rather say that all humor has conflict.

Check this out. You will find that anything humorous, if not always hostile, is, without fail, based on conflict. Sometimes undisguised, unadorned, unabashed hostility is funny— as in Don Rickles. Humor isn't necessarily witty and wit isn't always humorous.

However, a little hostility never hurt anybody and wit tempers it at both the receiving and giving ends. (I have no documentation to back this up, but I don't believe any form of extreme cruelty could be perpetrated by anyone with a well-developed sense of humor.)

Charlie Chaplin's comedy was almost entirely physical for the obvious reason that it was mostly sight humor. What goes unnoticed, however, is that it was usually violent. The beginning of American humor was steeped in violence; the bladder-pounding the comic took in burlesque, the pratfall, the seltzer bottle, the pie in the face, the "pow" of comic strips. As the talkies came, our comedy became more erudite and verbal but still retained its appetite for violence, and as anyone who has been the victim of cutting witticism knows, words can be violent, too.

A hack composer showed his maestro a requiem he had written for Schubert's funeral. The maestro read it and sighed sadly. "How much better all around it would have been," he said, "if you had died and Schubert had written the requiem."

So—if you don't like violence, if you don't want to hurt anybody, if you can't stand the sight of blood, you'd better look for another line of work. (The clergy is one that comes to mind, but with the hellfire and damnation in the next world and the competitive politics in this one, even that profession fails to qualify.) Not for the writer of humor is faint heart; caution, yes, but always in equal parts with daring.

One of the most potent manifestations of hostility is humiliation. Wits humiliate: comics allow themselves to be humiliated. Which is why you may admire the wit but you are more at ease with the comic. If you want to be the life of the party, drop your pants, spill wine over yourself, tell them how you can't make it with the opposite sex, how terrible your spouse treats you, how awful you look, how clumsy you are, and they'll not only laugh, but they'll love you for it.

The insult is an easy form of humor. That's because a "no holds barred . . . catch as catch can" form of confrontation is often allowable in comedy, where it would be disapproved in any other situation. Also because another of our unattractive traits we like to sweep under the rug called human nature, is that we usually enjoy the discomfiture of others. (Probably because we're relieved that we aren't the targets.) Thornton Wilder said, "We all like to see our best friend kicked downstairs." But only in comedy can we allow ourselves that gratification.

At script meetings on my first comedy show, the star received the most gratifying response to his ad libs because his insults were unrestricted and the laughs obligatory. The producer received the second most, because he could insult everybody except the star. The top writer could only rank up there if he was really witty, since the producer and star were out of bounds. And so it went down the pecking order to me, who could be funny only about noncontroversial subjects like the coffee or the secretary. (Only rarely did I ever try, because once I dared take the spotlight, I was fair prey to everybody except the secretary. And later even without that exception—she had something going with the producer.)

It was amazing, as I rose up the ladder, how much wittier I became. Once I had my own show, I could get laughs on brilliant lines such as "Hold the mayonnaise." The day I resigned, I remember, I sneezed and in a room full of people who had laughed at my mayonnaise line, not one said gesundheit.

Hostility is usually acceptable if it's witty. Obscenity is tolerated only if it's witty. Weakness is adored if it's witty. (Woody Allen has made a career of it.) Even ignorance is attractive if it's witty. As a matter of fact, a good rule of thumb is that you can do or say anything if you can get a laugh while you are doing or saying it. Which is why many people would rather be funny than President.

On the other hand, those in authority don't have to be witty. If they do try, it's just for fun. We others do if we want to stay around. We do it for survival. There's plenty of rest for the wicked; it's the oppressed who have to keep dancing. And that goes especially for comedy writers.

Laughter does not necessarily have any relationship to wit, humor, or comedy. We laugh when we are nervous, when we are embarrassed, when we are frightened. We laugh in relief, also. When someone falls down, looks ridiculous, acts stupid, or is especially uncouth, we laugh because we are relieved it isn't happening to us.

So wit, a more acceptable reason to laugh at the above unhumorous situations, is doubly welcome. We adults no longer laugh (presumably) at speech or physical handicaps, because we've learned better manners, and, more important, learned to empathize and to care. Nevertheless, some comics and some comedy writers utilize these unfunny substitutes for humor when they are insecure about the wit content of their offering.

In humor, nothing is sacred; not ethnic groups, not religion, not mother, not the flag, not God. These targets are especially vulnerable to bad taste, however, when stereotypes are exploited rather than satirized. This is when comedy is written by the numbers, unimaginative, predigested. It is not good comedy, sometimes not any kind of comedy and, at its worst, offensive.

Insensitive humor directed toward minorities, for example, gets its laughs from people who have a larger investment in the prejudice than they have appreciation of the humor. Effective humor sneaks behind prejudices, cuts through pretensions, avoids compromises, and bursts through restraints, until it finds its target in the pure, unpolluted human nature underneath.

A friend of mine was traveling through Chicago where my family lived and offered to call my mother, whom she'd never met, to extend my regards. She called, and this is the way the conversation went:

> *My mother: "Hello."*
> *My friend: "Mrs. Saks?"*
> *My mother: "Yes."*
> *My friend: "My name is Louise Colbert. You don't know me."*
> *My mother: "Then why are you calling?"*

I have told the story many times. and could always depend on the response of a gratifying laugh.

Consider: If someone were to call you on the phone and say, "My name is Louise Colbert, you don't know me," your inevitable next thought would be, then why are you calling? Then what makes the line so funny?

We have many automatic unacknowledged reactions, and their sudden expression will elicit a combination of identification plus relief that it was not we who were so foolish as to express it. (So-called humor by children is usually the articulation of an obvious reaction that the adult is too devious to express.)

And while we are on the subject, two similar incidents that occurred to friends who share my profession:

Milt Josefsberg was writing for Jack Benny when the comedian was going to New York and offered to call Milt's family while there. Milt, knowing how thrilled his mother would be to talk personally with the star, readily accepted the offer.

The conversation:

Mrs. Josefsberg: "Hello."

Jack Benny: "Mrs. Josefsberg?"

Mrs. Josefsberg: "Yes."

Jack Benny: "This is Jack Benny."

Mrs. Josefsberg: "And I'm Clark Gable."

Bob Schiller relates this interchange by his parents.

Mrs. Schiller to her husband: "If you die before me, how would you like to be buried?"

Father: "Surprise me."

(This same writer opens his talks to aspiring scribes with the words, "There are no good comedy writers. Only bad parents.")

Complete nonsense is always pleasurable, but is usually disdained by adults as immature. It takes a secure adult to laugh at it—and courage of heroic proportions to perform it. Steve Martin's arrow through the head, for example, and his "I'm a wild and crazy guy" get an appreciative response for the charming, almost childlike disavowal of both logic and self-consciousness.

Anything pretentious or hypocritical is fertile ground for humor. Instance: Americans have traditionally refused to acknowledge publicly any normal bodily functions, such as elimination and intercourse. (Even perspiring is acknowledged only in euphemistic terms. *"Horses* sweat," I remember being corrected as a child when I hadn't yet learned to be devious. "Men perspire, and women are all aglow.")

We refer to restrooms, bathrooms, powder rooms, ladies' rooms, but never to what they really are— toilets. (It's a little startling to hear a sixty-year-old grandmother giggle that she must go to the little girl's room.)

Ass, toilet, urinate, breasts, penis, etc. were never referred to in polite society except scientifically, and even then
sometimes further camouflaged in Latin to protect the innocent.
(Remember Kraft-Ebbing, the classical reference book on sexual aberrations, which would resort to Latin just when it came
to the good part?)

My generation was brought up to act, in mixed company,
as though we were all built like Barbie dolls. No sex, no genitals, not even secondary erogenous zones. By mutual consent,
both sexes acted as though that was a violin case the woman was
carrying on her chest under her clothes. Until very recently,
words like pregnant, virgin, menstrual, rape (even sex, unless it
referred only to gender) were never found in family publications.

Humor has done much to eliminate misleading euphe-
misms as well as unwieldy inhibition. Like a heat-seaking mis-
sile, it finds and attacks hypocrisy.

*"After five years of analysis, I've finally overcome my Oedipus
complex. Now I can say fuck to my m...o...t...h...e...r."*

Humor is used so that we don't have to spell out either of
these two awesome words. A minor benefit is the elimination of
the blank letters for verboten words. They usually only served
to exaggerate the offensiveness by provoking us to fit in the
proper obscenity—d---, s---, m----- f-----. (See, now you're
doing it, too.)

In polite society, the bodily functions could only be ex-
pressed in the camouflage of diminutive or foreign phrases, as
though only a child or foreigner could be excused for being
tasteless. Which is why such a large field of American comedy
was toilet or sex jokes. (Remember, as a child, the uncontrolla-
ble hilarity at any reference to the unmentionable body functions?)

Humor is as real, as honest, as human as suffering. Just as
the history of evolution can be followed by fossils, the history

of discrimination can be followed by the jokes of each era. First the Irish, then the Blacks, Jews, Italians, lately the Poles, Hispanics, etc. These are only the ethnic minorities, of course. Other minorities that served as the butt of comedy included the short, the fat, the impotent, the homosexual, the stupid, the ugly, etc., etc. Sometimes, for the purpose of convenience, a characteristic is coupled with a nationality; e.g., the Irish are hard drinkers, the Scotch are stingy, the Jews are grasping, the Blacks are illiterate, male interior decorators are homosexual . . . offensive examples seem nauseatingly endless. This is the result as much of laziness in character description as of bigotry. More admirable and gratifying is the historical use of humor by the oppressed themselves to alleviate intolerable persecution.

For years we heard jokes based on the patronizing premise that Blacks loved, above all else, watermelon. Then the counterattack. Jokes were made about people who believed that Blacks loved, above all else, watermelon. An example of how comedy is used to nurture prejudice and then used to destroy that very same prejudice.

When Dick Gregory, the black comedian, for the first time ever told a white audience of the black perception of them, he made a giant step for black equality. When women and homosexuals, in their worthy, unequal, and so far serious fight for equality start to use humor in their battle, they will begin to outflank the enemy. There is evidence that the cannons are being wheeled into position. For instance, the war cry displayed on a well-rounded T-shirt that reads, *A woman needs a man like a fish needs a bicycle.*

Jokes by the victims themselves are sensitive as well as purposeful. We use wit to enlist the help of a third party against an antagonist.

Ridicule is a powerful weapon. When used insensitively it is often cruel. When used against injustice it can bring the malefactor to his knees quicker than physical force.

Humor is a great weapon, certainly, but how do you create comedy out of such disagreeable subjects as prejudice, bigotry, persecution, hypocrisy, injustice, etc.?

First you get their attention.

Start by choosing a provocative subject. This is very important. As important as the farmer picking the right soil for his crop. No matter how expert he is, or how hard he works, he'll have a better harvest from good fertile bottomland. A provocative subject is one that is compelling, within the realm of your audiences' experiences or pertaining to their fears and dreams. In short, one that will pique their interest.

It is also usually one that is familiar and controversial. The clerk makes jokes about the customers. Army humor is almost always directed toward the ranking superior. Students gibe about teachers, while the teaching profession is often made tolerable by pointed barbs in the faculty lounge.

When you've got them where you want them, you can view that injustice from a new angle, strip it of its protective covering, perhaps exaggerate to show it in its absurdity. And if that unexpected resolution can also show how the prejudice is stupid, persecution intolerable, bigotry laughable, etc., you have provided the laugh you were brought there for, and struck a small blow against injustice in the bargain.

It is apparent to anyone that to find something tragic about an incident, situation, or person, one must feel concerned. What is not so apparent is that to find something humorous or comic in an incident, situation, or person, one must feel equally concerned.

Humor is used for feelings that are too deep for tears. It can bring to light things that can hurt as well as delight—and once they are brought to light, they never seem to hurt as much.

Very early in my career, the dropping of the bomb on Hiroshima gave me three different and separate shocks. The first was the horror of this new death-dealing invention. The second shock was a few weeks later when I heard, with revulsion, a joke about that same horrendous weapon. My third shock was a few years later when I found myself writing a joke about the atom bomb.

Comedy is no more superficial, trivial, or ineffectual than

tragedy. Very often quite the opposite. But for some reason, to the dismay of humorists, it is often relegated to the confectionery department of our culture, which is why comics want to play Hamlet.

Tell a joke that isn't funny and it will be greeted with derision; tell one that's been told before and it will be met with an accusatory reminder; but tell a dull, repetitive, serious story and the listener bears his boredom and pain in silence. Sydney Cox, one of the outstanding teachers of writing, said, "There is no such thing as the quite successful comedian, just as there is no such thing as the quite successful God."

Certain things, places, names are funny. Usually because of identification, context, sound, or sometimes for reasons lost in the mists of creation. Brooklyn is funny, but Albany isn't (ironic, since many more ludicrous things happen in the state capital). Mother-in-law is funny but father-in-law isn't. Chevrolet is funny (Essex is hilarious, as Jack Benny proved, but the statute of limitations has run out on it) while Dodge isn't (a 1969 Chevrolet is funnier than an undated one but a 1969 Dodge gets more serious). Ass is funny, as in fall on your . . . and kick your. . . . And boobs are funny, but shoulders and thighs aren't. (If you think it's because they're sexual, note: the genitals are not funny and like the 1969 Dodge, the more specific you get the more serious it becomes.) Texas is funny but Wyoming isn't (as a matter of fact, the only challenge to the State of Texas in the comedic sweepstakes is California, which tries hard but runs a poor second because it also arouses hostility). A cocker spaniel is funny, a German shepherd isn't. . . .

No need to belabor the point, but before we leave it, specificity is always funnier. Albany, or a cocker spaniel, is funnier than simply saying a city or a dog. For instance:

"I tried to drive my car between two oncoming trucks. Anybody want to buy a tall, thin Chevrolet?" is sharper than, *"Anybody want to buy a tall, thin automobile?"*

There are certain very unreliable judges as to what is funny.

One of the most unreliable is the cast. The rehearsal stage is, next to a reading of an epic poem in blank verse in a foreign language, the most boring of experiences. A stranger walking onto the rehearsal stage will find herself the center of attention, heads swiveling toward her entrance in the effort to cut through the tedium.

A great danger in comedy is that after the repetition of rehearsals, the lines may sound unfresh, unoriginal, and unfunny. That is when the lines heard by the audience may not be the best but merely the latest.

In that excruciatingly dull environment, any new line or piece of stage business is welcome relief, and almost guaranteed to get an enthusiastic reaction. Actors who will listen stone-faced to the carefully honed, original line read for the fortieth time, will collapse in paroxysms of laughter at an obvious, irrelevant, but new line substituted by a bored bit player. The onlooking writer's frustration turns to dismay when he hears the director say, "That's great! Leave it in."

"Those lines weren't written on the bus on the way over here," I heard a writer grumble when he saw them arbitrarily changed. But they finally may have been written by a bored prop man who has run out of comic books and is trying to impress a cute extra.

Typists are also notoriously bad judges of what's funny. They are usually too involved in their own responsibilities and trying to decipher the penciled-in changes to be amused. I remember one who typed page after page of what I thought were some very witty lines without even so much as a smile. Then finally I heard an explosive, welcome laugh.

"What . . . what . . . what?" I asked.

"Look at the way you spelled excruciating," she chortled.

Those with whom we may be involved in meaningful relationships are also undependable judges. Their reaction is too dependent on how the relationship is going and whether its warranty time has expired.

Then there are the buyers of our wares, whose judgment is sometimes unreliable but always unavoidable. However, the fact that their primary concern is the commercialization of the project is not necessarily a drawback.

We are all trying to reach as broad an audience as possible. The danger is that executives tend to look upon the creative artists as children. We are sometimes children. So are they. So is everybody. That's why laughing and making people laugh is so gratifying. We give way to the child in ourselves and appeal to the child in others. And, despite the potential reward of the five-bathroom house with an ermine-lined swimming pool, that's where most of the gratification lies.

Curiously enough, some of the more reliable judges are nonprofessionals, partly because they are not competitive and have nothing at stake to influence them. However, once you make the mistake of telling them they're good critics, or borrow money from them, they lose their effectiveness.

Mothers and spouses may be unsophisticated, but they are also uncorrupted. And you *know* they're on your side. I've often seen a successful, experienced writer, actor, or producer leave a roomful of highly paid experts to get the opinion of someone with no qualifications but a caring love.

One of my first jobs writing comedy was the old "Duffy's Tavern" radio show. A man named Abe Burrows was what we then called the head writer, and he handed me back my first submission with the admonition, "It needs punching up."

Embarrassed to confess my ignorance to him, I asked a more experienced friend, "What does punching up mean?"

"It means," my friend said, "that he wants you to make it funnier."

"Does he think," I asked incredulously, "that I could have written it funnier and *didn't*?"

Actually, yes. They always think you can make it funnier but perversely won't. And what makes it even more burdensome is that when you are in those depths of despair that writers slide into so easily, you believe they are right.

They aren't, you know. They never are. The only one who is right is you and sometimes, on beautiful and too rare occasions, the audience.

·3·

Anatomy of a Joke

*"If you don't understand,
don't mess with it.
If it works,
don't analyze it."*

There is a theory that jokes are made by men in prison. I'm not sure of the accuracy of that statement, but many are made by people who should be there. Jokes, however, are almost always made of, by, and for the oppressed.

That funny, perfectly fashioned joke your friend told you last night did not come into existence full blown, like Adam in the Garden of Eden. Instead, it followed Darwin's theory of natural selection. It started as simply a playful judgment of something incongruous. If it had merit, it was repeated. Each interpretation was slightly different. The embellishments that improved the story were kept in the next interpretation, those that didn't atrophied and dropped off. The result is that carefully honed, economically worded, well-made joke you heard last night.

As a youngster, I recall that my two great anxieties were not to smell bad and not to be a sissy. To cover my vulnerability I made jokes. When I realized that every other boy had the same fears, I was on my way to becoming a writer.

Everybody needs to be a star at some time or other. And if we can't do it any other way, we'll wear a lamp shade for a hat, enter a cake at the county fair, try a double gainer off the diving board, offer to fight any man in the bar, or tell jokes. The last is by no means the least dangerous. To some of us, it's the only way left. It's the same reason why the underprivileged, seven-foot, gangly boy from the ghetto goes out for basketball. How else could he get noticed for something other than being very tall?

Notice how rarely the star pitcher or football player tries for a laugh? He doesn't have to. Remember when the girl described as ". . . a lot of fun at a party" was almost inevitably unattractive? She felt she needed something else going for her.

Mel Brooks describes himself as "the kid who was always sliding into second base." Neil Simon, on the other hand, freely admits to writing jokes, as such, only rarely. Other examples to document this point are Woody Allen, Paul Mazursky, Dick Cavett, Larry Gelbart, who started their careers writing jokes.

Jokes might be called the building blocks of comedy. I believe Neil Simon does write jokes. So did Dickens and Shakespeare. When they are used inside the format of a story, they take on another, more subtle form. The good joke does not have an obvious "straight" line to set up the joke. At their most skillful, jokes are like seasoning in gourmet cooking—indistinguishable, but adding so much to the taste.

There are, of course, no specific directions, as insert A into B in putting together a coaster wagon. As a matter of fact, there are probably no rules or directions at all. Analyzing to see what makes something funny can be likened to pulling off the petals of a rose to find out what makes it beautiful. But to the writer of comedy and the artist, respectively, such experiments may be of benefit.

The ingredients of comedy are, not necessarily in the order of importance, simplicity, clarity, relevance, exaggeration, surprise, irreverence, incongruity, identification, precision, and, by all means—by all possible means—rhythm.

We are aware of the importance of timing in humor, but sometimes unaware that it is only part of the overall use of *rhythm*. Good prose has a subtle rhythm, especially in dialogue. In very good prose—Shakespeare, Hemingway, Steinbeck, for example—it's almost poetry. It's very important in any kind of writing. In humor it's not only essential, but perhaps as necessary as it is in poetry and song.

The difference between the rhythm in other forms of prose and the rhythm in comedy is like the difference between the motor in an automobile and a single-engine airplane. They are basically similar, but if the motor fails in your car you get a lift or walk home. If it fails in your plane, you crash. (Although stuttering and pauses can be an advantage—Woody Allen, the veteran Joe Frisco, and Jack Benny readily come to mind—when they are used so expertly that they add to the rhythm.)

The mildest of witticisms becomes more effective when offered in rhythm. I remember working with a comedian who had excellent rhythm but poor judgment. At times, he would misinterpret an exposition line as a joke and read it with comedic rhythm. To our continual surprise, this reading of a serious line in comedy rhythm would inevitably draw a laugh. In further substantiation, a joke told in actual *rhyme* (as in greeting cards, for example) always seems funnier.

In researching this chapter, I interviewed both writers and performers about timing in comedy. My question of how one learned the use of rhythm and timing was usually met with a shrug. It was like asking an old-fashioned cook how much salt to use. "Just enough and not too much," would probably be the answer.

The only way to achieve rhythm, the above masters eventually agreed, was through "feel," an instinctive facility mastered only through experience. That's why comedians must learn their trade in front of an audience. The writer also learns by experience, but you will get a quicker and more accurate feel if you will—as I, and I expect most experienced writers of comedy do—read your lines aloud.

"Who was that lady I saw you with last night?"

"That woman was not a lady. She happens to have been my wife."

Now feel the easy, smooth rhythm in:

"That was no lady. That was my wife."

Granted, economy and precision are also evident here, but all are used to help make the rhythm.

There is no magic formula to attain it. Just as the aforementioned cook puts in a pinch of this and that and keeps tasting until it is just right, the writer of a comedy line keeps saying it over and over until it has a smooth, easy rhythm.

Clarity and *simplicity* are, again, desirable in all writing, but necessary in comedy. They are crucial ingredients because in comedy you *must* have your audience's undivided attention. If they puzzle over a word or thought ever so slightly, if they are distracted by an unnecessary word or phrase, you lose their concentration and the temperamental comedy disappears in a huff. An actor, by the simple gesture of lighting a cigarette, can steal the scene from another who has all the good lines. A comedian who stumbles, even preceding the joke, will start again from the beginning, or more likely discard the joke entirely. Comedy is delicate, but when nurtured and handled properly, can have the grace of a rapier and the power of a cannonball.

The best comedy has *precision,* which, put simply, is the exact word in its proper place. It is highly desirable and usually in short supply, but it can be learned. It takes patience, an extensive vocabulary, plus the above-mentioned characteristics of clarity and simplicity. S.J. Perelman and James Thurber are examples of master craftsmen who placed words with the deftness and art of a poet or songwriter.

Identification is also a valuable tool in comedy. Used by writers in the sense of "to identify with," identification means the listener or reader can relate to your characters.

This isn't as circumscribed as it sounds. A middle-aged, white, automobile mechanic does not relate only to middle-aged, white, automobile mechanics. He may relate to a king, a black housewife, an oversexed elephant, or an oak tree, if it can talk or think. Just so long as the character has problems or dreams he has experienced.

When your audience can identify with the character, then everything that happens to the character happens to them, and you, the writer, have that omnipotent influence on the mood of others that all artists dream of.

Close to identification are the qualities of the familiar and recognizable, comfortable and friendly elements that can make laughter so much more readily forthcoming. An experienced speaker at a banquet will often research that specific place and name buzz words that will get the reaction of recognition. (A stranger, hearing a line such as, "And Bill Forrester can usually be found near the Coke machine in the accounting department," will be mystified at the uproarious laugh that follows.) Bob Hope used this device with equal success at army camp shows, and often equal mystification from the television audience. Some of our present-day comedians—Bill Cosby and Alan King are examples—have made this into a fine art.

The closer you can get to universal emotions or problems, the better chance you have to win identification. If you have a problem in your own home about who carries out the garbage, notice how your interest sharpens at the mere mention of the problem of carrying out the garbage. Erma Bombeck does wonders with bringing up problems that relate to her readers. And because they are everyday problems that are happening right now they have the further advantage of being *relevant*. (Also note that she takes the problems on herself, which not only makes it easier for us to bear them, but easier for us to love her.)

The identification, recognition, and relevancy inherent in very common problems . . . "The other day a cop stopped me for going through a light. . . . Well, here it is income tax time. . . . I decided to ask my boss for a raise. . . ." bring a camaraderie and anticipatory smile at their very mention.

Misfortune, fear, prejudice, pomposity, inadequacy, and conceit are the fertile soils out of which we cultivate comedy; identification, exaggeration, incongruity, irreverence, and surprise, its most potent fertilizers.

Exaggeration and *incongruity* are first cousins, and by their very nature lend themselves to humor. We loved them as children and we find them just as delightful now. We are charmed at the premise of the elephant who falls in love with the sparrow, and intrigued by the man who hasn't spoken to his wife for forty years. Humor gives us the license. We can have a woman two hundred years old, or a man with carrots growing out of his head. When a man is punched he winds up in the hospital, or he is the world's greatest lover, or so ugly he haunts houses for a living . . . our audience not only allows exaggeration, they welcome it.

So, be bold. In comedy there is much less danger in going too far than there is in not going far enough.

Surprise is vital in the storytelling art. If we knew exactly what was coming, we wouldn't have to read, watch, or listen. And comedy, from the two-line joke to the feature picture is, as we have pointed out before and will probably point out again, storytelling. Except that in comedy the surprise is sharper and quicker.

We must go from what audiences know to something they didn't expect, and point out a resolution they never thought of. We can assume that unless we tell them something they don't expect, we can never get the spontaneous laugh, chuckle, or even bemused smile we're paid to deliver.

A strong ally to surprise in comedy is misdirection. We achieve misdirection by establishing the familiar, pointing toward the predictable . . . and then opening the trapdoor. If it is done with dexterity, and without cheating, your audience will be as charmed as children seeing magic, delighted at being fooled, and climb out of the trapdoor with smiles on their faces.

In creating the humorous line or situation, the writer first establishes an identifiable situation. He will then do well to try to think of the obvious and predictable answer his audience expects—in order to be sure not to give it to them. He may even go so far as to leave false clues to lead the audience astray. Then with that obvious, predictable answer as a springboard, he can use incongruity, exaggeration, irreverence (the surprise comes built in) to get his laugh.

Deference, respect, and reverence are antidotes to humor. You will have great trouble being funny if you are influenced by any of those characteristics. Comedy, by its very definition, is irreverent, disrespectful, and defers to no person or institution.

Politeness is also inhibiting to comedy. *Irreverence* entails fearlessness and resistance to conformity, two very productive qualities in writing funny lines. Humor itself is a trampling over boundary lines, rebellion against social standards, and usually takes an adversary position.

Obviously, fear and conformity, handmaidens of reverence and deference, make humor difficult if not impossible. That is why the humor in totalitarian countries is almost always underground.

All comedy is storytelling, from the pratfall to the full-length play or feature picture. All comedy, as all drama, has conflict, and all comedy, as all drama, is based on the *three-act construction*. There are many, many definitions and descriptions of the three-act construction. George M. Cohan's was: "In the first act you get your hero up a tree; the second act you throw rocks at him; third act you let him down"—which is as good a definition as any.

Every humorous anecdote, every two-line joke, is a story and follows the three-act construction—situation, development, resolution.

Take Henny Youngman.

"Take my wife . . . please." This joke may be eligible for the *Guinness Book of Records* by having three acts in four words. "Take my wife," establishes that he has a wife and is going to talk about her, for the first act. "Please" may set another record for having two acts in one word. It is the second act in that it tells us that he cannot tolerate his wife. It then simultaneously becomes the third act by changing the meaning of the first, surprising and delighting us in the process by the deft word legerdemain.

The first act, or straight line, as it's called in comedy, establishes the situation and characters. In the pretelevision days of the stand-up comics, before the electronic flood of entertainment, when comedy material could be used over and over, the jokes usually came equipped with ready-made first acts.

Remember . . .

There was this Jewish rabbi, Protestant minister, and Catholic priest. . . .

A man stopped another man on the street and said, "Can you spare a dime for a cup of coffee?" And the man said. . . .

• • •

This traveling salesman's car broke down and he walked to a nearby farmhouse and asked if he could spend the night. The farmer said to him. . . .

• • •

This man walked into the bar with a parrot on his shoulder and said to the bartender. . . .

• • •

The man called the waiter over and said, "Waiter, there's a fly in my soup." . . .

• • •

A man went to register at a hotel. The clerk said, "I'm sorry we have no rooms left, but. . . .

And then the ever-popular, no-frills, off-the-rack—

My husband is so stingy that. . . .
My wife is so stupid that. . . .
My girlfriend is so fat that. . . .

First acts all. Still sometimes used by a type of comedian of which Henny Youngman is probably the best known. The reason they were so popular is the same reason we call it stand-up comedy. The comedian was starting from scratch. No situation, no character except the comedian's baggy pants and putty nose to let you know he intended to be funny. So each joke must needs have its own situation and persona—the first act—which, like disposable diapers, could be used only once and discarded.

An example of the first steps toward more sophisticated humor might be Rodney Dangerfield's "I get no respect. . . ." There are other sophisticated practitioners—Joan Rivers, Alan King, Bill Cosby, et al, still using the same three-act construction, but they all bring their own custom-made, reusable first acts. (Phyllis Diller and her unattractiveness, and Bill Cosby's underprivileged youth, for instance.)

There are, of course, many more complicated and subtle ingredients to the humor of these fine comedians. But for the purposes of this laboratory example, we are only concerned with the skeleton.

Now let's add the second act—the development.

There was this Jewish rabbi, Protestant minister and Catholic priest (second act) *in a lifeboat that could hold only one person. . . .*

• • •

A man died and went to heaven and when he got to the pearly gates, St. Peter said to him, (second act) *"Tell me one reason why I should let you through. . . ."*

• • •

The farmer said to the traveling salesman, (second act) *"I have no extra bed, but I have a daughter who. . . ."*

• • •

My girlfriend is so fat (second act) *that when she steps on a scale. . . ."*

Then the third act—better known as the punch line. That's why they sent for you.

The third act is the resolution, basically the same in comedy as it is in any form of writing. It only differs, as stated before, in mood and attitude. The unorthodox point of view, exaggeration, surprise; that's where the comedy writer earns his money. Do it with originality, flair, and courage and you're a success. Do it competently and you'll still make a living. Leave out the unexpected, unorthodox point of view and you're writing drama. Which isn't bad unless you had other plans.

Let's demonstrate with the example from Chapter 2. A beautiful day, a pretty girl, a good meal—the first act. The second act—it rains, you have no money for the check, and the waiter steals your girl. Now we come to the crucial third act.

Whether it's a joke, a monologue, a newspaper column, a screen play, or a book, the basic comedy construction for the third act is the same—the unorthodox point of view, the unexpected denouement. Let's try it as a joke first.

"What did you do?"

"What could I do? I promised to send him his tip in the mail."

Or:

"That girl sounds terrible."

"Oh, she wasn't so bad. She asked him to drop me at the bus stop."

Or:

"At least you learned a lesson."

"I sure did. Always carry an umbrella, don't leave home without American Express, and eat only in cafeterias." (Okay, okay. At least you get the idea.)

A note of caution: Don't go on after the punch line. Comedy writers call it "Going past the post office." Dramatic writers call it anticlimactic. You have reached your destination and going on, unless, of course, you're on your way to another joke, is like keeping the motor running after you're home. It is an inconvenience, without any rewards, that only dissipates the pleasure of the trip.

The *monologue* has basically the same construction with the add-a-joke facility, still using, of course, the same first and second acts. It also has the feature of allowing you to segue, when you feel you have mined a particular subject, to another related topic. Such as:

"I always seem to get that kind of girl. Like the one who excuses herself to go to the powder room, and after waiting an hour and a half I realize she meant the one in her home."

Or:

"I don't know if my mother would like the kind of girl I'd bring home. I could never get them that far."

Then, after that vein is mined out we could move to:

"Now that I'm married things are different. My wife and I have an agreement. I've promised to go out only with the fellows and she promised the same thing."

The monologue, then, is made up of a series of interrelated

three-act jokes, told by one person in anywhere from the five-minute Bob Hope or Johnny Carson opening, to the fifteen or twenty minutes of a nightclub act, all the way to the hour-and-a-half of a complete Richard Pryor show.

Comics usually try to finish with their strongest joke. It's a real achievement to bow off during a big laugh. But if there are any sure-fire jokes, there are no sure-fire audiences. An older device, not much used today, was to end with a song. Today, the comic will usually avoid the challenge by a simple, "Thank you very much." Sometimes preceded by an ingratiating, "You've been a wonderful audience."

Sketch comedy, which is a broad situation in one scene (probably originated, as much comedy has, from burlesque) is used today mostly in variety shows and revues. It will have an overall third act, in the sense that all the plot and joke lines lead toward the same resolution.

The classic burlesque sketch, "For God's sake, pay him the two dollars" for instance, which was predicated on a lawyer stubbornly appealing and reappealing his client's two dollar traffic citation, lasted for five to ten minutes of jokes and scenes all leading to the punchline (third act) of the client going to the electric chair.

Print comedy—periodical columns and books, most often personal reminiscences—usually has an understated third act, but it's there, nevertheless. In comic strips it's in the last panel, and in comedy greeting cards it's on the inside. *Theatrical, cinema, or television comedy* follows the same rules of technique as drama.

Before we go on, two important notes: I happen to have picked for my example the fall guy type of humor, the category so well utilized by such as Woody Allen, Jackie Gleason's lost soul, and Rodney Dangerfield. It goes without saying that there are many other areas for humor (such as situation, mistaken identity, satirical) but they are all subject to the same basic construction.

The second point is that I am demonstrating the three-act construction only for purposes of analysis. It would be counterproductive for the writer, while trying to create the funny line or situation, to inhibit the creative flow by consciously conforming to the rules of construction and techniques. It should be used only if the comedy isn't working. It may be said more than once in this book, but it bears repeating, especially for comedy: If it works, don't analyze it; if you don't understand it, don't mess with it.

At its best, the construction of comedy is like the magician's trap door and the gears under the carousel—invisible. There is no apparent first act. It is buried and expertly camouflaged in the situation and character. The most gratifying laugh is the one you get from something that doesn't sound like a joke, that has no obvious straight line, that is a natural, seemingly random line. But this seemingly random line is securely fastened to strong invisible foundations.

The most difficult and ineffectual way to write a joke (or a story, or play, or novel, for that matter), is to try to provide a third act for a prefabricated first and second act. The most desirable and successful way is for the writer to provide all three acts. That is when he can pick a situation and characters that are appealing to him, provide them with an identifiable problem and resolve it in an amusing way. That is the method the masters of the craft, such as Richard Pryor, Woody Allen, and Neil Simon will, I believe, agree is their preferred method.

In the early days of radio and television comedy, producers would sometimes try to team a jokester with no sense of construction with a craftsman with no sense of humor, hoping to get good comedy, well constructed. As usually happens with the creative efforts of management, it ended disastrously. The result was unsuccessful comedy, poorly constructed. (Reminiscent of the old story of when Isadora Duncan suggested to George Bernard Shaw that they have a baby together.

"Just think," she proposed, "of a baby with your brains and my looks."

"Just think," he refuted, via his usual postcard, "of a baby with my looks and your brains.")

But, just as the same simple step is fundamental to every movement of the waltz, so the same three-act construction is basic to all comedy. Let me offer an example. Shortly after the second world war, when the United States was helping rehabilitate Japan and Germany, this story came out of Israel:

A high functionary came to Prime Minister Ben-Gurion with a plan to get Israel out of its desperate economic plight.

"We'll declare war on the United States," he proposed. "And then, after we lose, they'll have to support us."

"Brilliant," Ben-Gurion answered. Then after further thought, he shook his head. "We can't take the chance," he said. "What if we win?"

As you see, the three acts are clearly apparent, but their real potential was not. The above few lines were made into a successful feature motion picture called *The Mouse That Roared*. That same simple three-act joke was amplified into 120 minutes of funny, relevant, engrossing comedy.

When I was a rookie on the radio show, "Duffy's Tavern," they had also hired, on a trip to New York, a promising new writer in his twenties. His name was Bill Manhoff and he later built a solid reputation for some of our best comedy, including the hit stage play, *The Owl and the Pussycat*. Before we returned to California, Bill recommended his erstwhile partner, also in his early twenties (*everybody* was in his early twenties in those days) to fill another opening on our staff. (Just as a *covey* of quail or a *pride* of lions, in our field it was called a *stable* of writers.)

Bill's partner submitted a sample of his work, and although the consensus was that he wrote literate and amusing lines, they were too "light" for the show. (Comedy that brings only amused smiles has a very short life span in prime time.)

So, while the rest of us "Chiefed" (as was said in those days) back to California, he was unhappily left back in New

York. While waiting for the security of an assignment, he tried his hand at musical comedy and subsequently wrote, *Paint Your Wagon, An American In Paris, Camelot, My Fair Lady,* etc.

The point, I guess, is that if Alan Jay Lerner had been able to write stronger punch lines, he might today be a successful television comedy writer.

·4·

That Damned Third Act

*"Imagining is creating
and illusions are its most
rewarding product."*

"Tell me a story. . . ." We never outgrow that hunger. Only many of the people who are saying it are now middle-aged and able to pay more than a candy-smudged kiss; five dollars for a movie, for example, fifteen dollars for a novel, and thirty dollars for the theater, to hear one. And if you can gratify that hunger, you can afford to get your daughter's teeth straightened, possibly a table at Ma Maison, and almost certainly suggestions as to how you could have told it better.

We are basically storytellers, descendants of the old men who sat around the fire and told us legends, fairytales, exploits, or maybe just how funny Og looked when he fell into the tar pit. Taking their place with the anticipatory pleasures of the smell of good food and sexual foreplay are those exciting words, "Once upon a time. . . ."

A dramatic writer tries to give momentary release from loneliness, the humorist tries to give momentary relief from despair; and if either is successful, the reward is a momentary feeling of power.

Art is the manipulation of someone else's imagination. That is why the artist, whether he is a bumbling Woody Allen, or a vulnerable, sensitive poet, must always be in control.

Pick a good story and tell it well—that's all there is to it. Be bold, be brief, be decisive, and speak out loudly.

And, be honest. James Cagney's advice to young actors bears repeating to young writers, "Plant your feet, look them in the eye, and tell the truth."

So, what is a good story? Where do you start and where do you end?

The last two are the easiest. You start at the beginning and end when you're finished. This is not a smart-ass answer. Start exactly where your story starts—not one word sooner—and stop when your story is told—not one word more. First, you need to know what it is you have to tell, what point you want to make, what your story is. Then start directly and clearly toward that goal.

A good story (or joke or sketch or poem) is any story a sufficient number of people are willing to take the time and pay the price to hear. Start by picking a story you think is a good story. That's what they came for. That's how you pay the rent. Go where they'll buy your wares, and try to give them what they're asking for. Within those boundaries, however, you can give it your best shot.

So pick material you like, because you'll do best at what you like best. And the most reliable measure of what others will think is funny is what you think is funny.

It's not infallible, but it's the only ruler you have with which to measure. Otherwise you're like a tone deaf musician trying to tune a violin. The artist must gamble that his audience will like the same things he does. So—with allowances for the changes, ramifications, and restrictions the middlemen ask for—if you miss the audience you are aiming at, you either have the wrong audience or it's the wrong bow and arrow.

Once you've succeeded in getting their interest, they will want to know how it comes out. They're waiting for the third act. First acts are easy; star-crossed lovers, the strange cowboy riding into town, the mysterious murder, the legendary diamond guarded by superstitious natives, etc. The second act is a little more difficult; the development of the problem presented in the first. But that damned third act . . .

The search for the third act has probably destroyed more writers than a high cholesterol count and drunk driving combined. Next to the agony of starting that first page, it may be the most difficult thing about writing. There are some very fine writers who didn't need third acts—Chekhov and Salinger are examples. But to us lesser writers who consider ourselves basically storytellers, it is of paramount importance.

Did you ever wonder why the strip-tease was more enthralling than simple nudity? It's because instant nudity has no third act.

People are continually saying, "My life could make a book." They're right—all it needs is a third act. Third acts in life are rare. So we have to make them up. The writer who can dream up the third act that is both gratifying and honest is the one they make cocktail parties for.

There are, in some types of stories, ready-made third acts. In a western, it's the shoot-out; in a love story, the consummation of the romance (until recently always leading to the obligatory wedding ceremony); in a sport event, the big game or the big fight; in a mystery, the congregation of suspects in the library. Notice I left out comedies? Because a comedy can be any of these.

There are many *ersatz* third acts; or perhaps a more accurate description is fake third acts. In television especially, it will often be a violent-somersaulting-jumping-over-chasms car chase. In these the writer has abdicated his responsibility to the stunt driver. Another common use of the ersatz third act is in the cops and robbers story. The criminal is unearthed and confronted, which would leave an unsatisfactory void if the story were to end there. Instead, somebody gets the drop, somebody loses the drop (it doesn't matter who or how) and we have the chase scene (are they *always* through underground parking areas, abandoned warehouses, roof-tops, or deserted amusement parks?) until the final capture. Then a quick fade out before anybody has a chance to say, "Third act? What third act? Wasn't there a third act? Oh well, it's too late now, we're already into the hairdresser and make-up credits."

So how do we get a third act? First, remember you want a resolution to the situation rather than just an ending. Look for what should happen, what could happen, or what might just possibly happen. Then tell it in a logical, dramatic, and compelling way. That should win the award in the "easier said than done" category. But that's where we earn our stripes. That's what separates us from those who just came to watch and listen.

There is, obviously, no sure-fire formula to finding that third act. It is so elusive, rare and perishable that I, and I'm sure many other professional writers, will not start the actual writing until I know I have it securely in stock. I am not content to have it on back order. Too often have I impetuously gone ahead with a delightful and interesting beginning to find myself up a blind alley, with no sign of an ending. As a matter of fact, I will usually work backward in this respect. If I have a sound third act, I know I can always manufacture a usable first and second.

(As an example, in the classic "I Love Lucy" series, the third act was always Lucy in a hilarious, usually physical predicament. The writers would almost always look for that comedic predicament first, then work backwards from it.)

No analysis of the storytelling technique would be complete without a discussion of the "message" picture.

Like the term "situation comedy," the message picture is a widely accepted misnomer. If the third act does *not* say virtue always triumphs, it is usually called a message picture.

"Let Western Union deliver the messages" takes its place with Winston Churchill's, "the soft underbelly of Italy" as a well-turned, effective, but inaccurate phrase.

First off, let's point out that the usual Western Union messages are to send money, or that your uncle just died, or congratulations on the opening of a new boutique. Necessary messages perhaps, but I for one am not willing to give them exclusive rights to the message industry.

Secondly, the so-called message pictures are simply those which delineate a situation that does not necessarily end happily—and do so without offering a judgment. Ironically, as soon as you point out the moral, such as "Mother knows best," "Crime does not pay," "Honesty is the best policy" (all of which are inaccurate at least some of the time) it takes it out of the message picture genre.

In every good story, every funny situation, we find in the third act a point of some kind. Most professional writers don't choose a moral, then try to find a story to fit. They look for a good story and if they find it, the point usually comes built-in. Dickens wrote whopping good tales exposing the abject poverty and inequitable legal system. Ibsen wrote excellent dramas of social significance. Which came first, the storytelling urge or the motivation to make a better world, we don't know. But it is interesting to note that long after the social inequities they described have disappeared, or at least improved, the stories remain as powerful and readable as ever.

"Man is an untiring pleasure seeker," someone once said. Some of us have chosen as our vocation to provide that pleasure. Other suppliers range all the way from the hooker to Beethoven. I'm not sure which end of that spectrum the comedy writer is closest to. I'm quite confident, however, that the best and worst of us are, at different times, close to both.

·5·

On Style

Proper words in proper places
make a true definition of a style.
JONATHAN SWIFT

Style (and originality perhaps) is really simple honesty. No one is exactly like you. No one feels exactly as you do. So . . . if you write with integrity, nothing will be exactly like it and there's your originality and your style. Comedy, written with graceful ease, is always readable, usually simple, and most always honest.

Style can be called the personality of your writing, and, like your own personality, it becomes awkward and dishonest if you are self-conscious about it. If you force it, it becomes stilted; if you are artificial, you lack style. If you write as clearly and honestly as you can, you can't help having style. Showing off, cheating, one-upmanship are poor style in any communication. In humor, it is as obvious as a wart on the end of your nose and as offensive as a punch in the mouth.

Those who disguise and deny their feelings are condemned for their deception to boredom and loneliness. They frustrate not only their loved ones but every artist who is trying to touch those feelings. Comedy writing at its best will not only entertain, but by exposing our common vulnerabilities, get us to acknowledge those feelings, and so, bring us back into the company of man.

Honesty in art is more than a virtue; it's an indispensable ingredient. It is not only the best policy, but has long ago displaced cleanliness in its position next to godliness. Except for getting out of boring social engagements I see no real profit in dishonesty, and even that exception may be invalid, since the same bores will probably reinvite you after the statute of limitations has run out on your fake headache.

Honesty is as important in the work of a comedy writer as it is in a bank president. Chekhov said that if a character is drawn properly he cannot say a false line. Examples are easier to see in mystery stories. If the clues are false, the story will fail. I don't mean misdirection, which is an acceptable and intriguing device in both mystery and comedy. I mean cheating. If you cheat, the delighted reaction won't be there in the mystery, the laugh will be lost in the comedy. In drama we call it weak construction. In comedy we call it a false straight line.

It is not cheating if you tell a story about a talking pig. We accept it with pleasant anticipation. Nobody says, "Wait a minute. Pigs don't talk." A charming aspect of all audiences is that they only want to know what they're to believe, and they'll give themselves up to it with an almost childlike trust. "A prince was turned into a frog. . . ." "There was this woman who lived in a chandelier. . . ." "A man with two heads walked into a bar. . . ." and we're with you. We see a bar and a man with two heads walking in, and we await the rest of the story with anticipatory delight.

But you'd damned well better tell us what happens with the prince who had turned into a frog. . . . and if you introduce us to a pig that talks, that articulate porcine had better provide the punch line.

Dishonesty will lose you the loyalty of your audience. And without that loyalty you won't get the laugh. And without the laugh, you might as well have stayed in bed.

Relevancy comes in the package with honesty. If you use an irrelevant line just because it's funny, it's dishonest writing, and you won't go to the comedy writers' heaven where the punch line always gets a laugh.

Working on comedy, writers will often be tempted by a funny line they know is untrue to the premise or character. The good writer resists the temptation. He knows that he will get that laugh only at the expense of the rest of the scene. Jack Benny played a miserly character who had a vault in his basement guarded day and night, a pay telephone in his home, etc., and we accepted it. But he could never deviate from that character without irreparable harm.

Relevancy means relating to the present characters and situations. There is an anecdote about a man who had only one story to tell, about the time that he had shot a bear. At every gathering he would somehow find an opening to get this story into the conversation. Except at one party, when he could find no way to bring it up. So, in the midst of the conversation, he suddenly ex-claimed, "What's that shot?" When the others all insisted there was no shot, he went on, "Well, since we're talking about shooting, let me tell you about the time I shot a bear. . . ."

He made his story relevant there and I'm making it rele-vant here.

Humor hasn't the time to be hypocritical, it hasn't the pa-tience to be polite, it hasn't the tolerance to be timid.

Drama can be 70, 60, or even 50 percent effective and be 70, 60, or 50 percent successful. Humor needs 100 percent ef-fectiveness or it lies there in ignoble defeat. If it doesn't work perfectly in every respect, if either timing or tone is one iota off, it is as unacceptable as music that is a half tone flat.

I have a personal prejudice against any picture where a character writes with a quill, or starts with a boy walking across a field, or begins with the dedication, "We wish to thank the United States Naval Academy for their cooperation. . . ." They seem to me to *promise* to be dull.

On the other hand, pictures that start with other clichés such as a cowboy riding into a strange town, a close-up of foot-steps walking on a nighttime sidewalk, a handsome couple of different sexes meeting for the first time, have the opposite ef-fect because they promise to at least try to avoid the predictable.

Clichés become clichés because they are effective. But they soon become predictable and boring, which is why we try to avoid them. If you have ever been to an art show or window shopping with someone much slower than you are, you are fa-miliar with the tedium of waiting for them to catch up.

If the audience knows what to expect, if they have to listen to information they've already heard, they will get restless. In comedy, you must give them information they don't have or an experience they don't anticipate. That's what makes it a crea-tive art.

There are thousands of ways to do a script and many of

them are right. The myth that there are no new stories is perpe-
tuated by those unable to create one. Actually—excepting those
plagiarized—there are no old ones. Like fingerprints or snow-
flakes, it is impossible to have two alike. It is not a miracle to
write a new story. The miracle would be if two people, no matter how close in age, viewpoint, temperament, or circumstance
were to write exactly the same story.

"Stick to the point and cut." Somerset Maugham said in a
few words what I've tried to say in a chapter. But it's important
enough to warrant a bit more nagging.

Just tell the story. That's style. When you try to look good
telling it, when you try to be cute, it is as if you're putting a
Christmas ornament on a blossoming apple tree.

Just tell the story. Just tell the goddamned story.

·6·

The Ten Commandments
Seven Deadly Sins
Four Essential Steps
and
Three Indispensable
Attributes
of Comedy Writing

THE TEN COMMANDMENTS
OF COMEDY WRITING

I. THOU SHALT BE BRIEF.

II. THOU SHALT BE SIMPLE.

III. THOU SHALT BE CLEAR.

IV. THOU SHALT BE BOLD.

V. THOU SHALT BE RELEVANT.

VI. THOU SHALT BE RECOGNIZABLE.

VII. THOU SHALT BE CONTROVERSIAL.

VIII. THOU SHALT BE UNPREDICTABLE.

IX. THOU SHALT BE ORIGINAL.

X. THOU SHALT BE SALABLE.

Those are the Shalts. Let's put in, for good measure, the Shaltnots.

XI. THOU SHALT NOT HONOR THY MOTHER OR FA-
THER OR ANY OTHER OF THY PREDECESSORS.

XII. THOU SHALT NOT BE COURTEOUS, REVERENT, OR
OBEDIENT.

XIII. THOU SHALT NOT HAVE A FALSE STRAIGHT LINE.

XIV. THOU SHALT NOT GO PAST THE PUNCH LINE.

XV. THOU SHALT NOT EXPLAIN.

XVI. THOU SHALT NOT APOLOGIZE.

XVII. THOU SHALT NOT BE INNOCUOUS.

XVIII.THOU SHALT NOT CONFORM.

XIX. THOU SHALT NOT BE TENTATIVE.

XX. THOU SHALT NOT BE UNTIMELY.

THE SEVEN DEADLY SINS
OF
COMEDY WRITING

1. TIMIDITY

2. DEFERENCE

3. OBSCURITY

4. POMPOSITY

5. BLANDNESS

6. BAD TIMING

7. IMITATION

Strangely, cruelty and viciousness are not among these, because things that are cruel and vicious to some are funny to others, and vice versa. Humor is democratic but not always fair. Also, not coincidentally, you may note that all the above sins are themselves nice, big, fat targets for humor.

THE FOUR ESSENTIAL STEPS
TO
WRITING COMEDY

1. PICK SOMETHING READILY IDENTIFIABLE.

2. ZERO IN ON THE CONFLICT.

3. TAKE AN UNCONVENTIONAL POINT OF VIEW.

4. SURPRISE US.

THE THREE INDISPENSABLE ATTRIBUTES
OF THE
COMEDY WRITER

1. MOTIVATION

2. COURAGE

3. HIGH TOLERANCE TO SUFFERING

·7·

Making the Decision

Who acts undertakes to suffer.
AESCHYLUS

A pause here, after these past pages of admonitions, warnings, and advice, for a well-earned respite of sympathy and encouragement.

Baby, it's cold out there. Writing is a continual succession of torturous decisions. The stories are all there, the scenes, the characters, the motivations, the words. It's choosing the right story, the right scene, the right motivations, the right words—and in the right order—that's the most difficult part of writing, as making the decision is probably the most difficult of any creative art. But make it you must, or find a less demanding line of work.

You have to get your ass on the seat, your hands on the typewriter, and go. You can't wait for the law of gravity to be abolished before you decide to jump. The only artists who aren't scared are the untalented ones. Live dangerously now or live wretchedly waiting for your rich uncle to die.

Edmund Kean, the noted actor, is reputed to have said on his deathbed, "Dying is easy, comedy is hard."

There's the sympathy.

Here's a soupçon of encouragement. You are already one of the elite when you've put it down on paper. Once you've made that decision and arranged words in an order that you think will amuse others, you have left behind that vast horde of people who plan to be writers as soon as they get around to it.

You have to be brave to take out that white sheet of paper and put on it words that could be evidence of your stupidity as well as your arrogance, to arrange those words on that paper in the hope they will entertain thousands, maybe millions—or maybe only two people—or nobody. The second bravest thing is to show it to somebody. The third most courageous is to show it without the apologetic, "Here's something I dashed off . . ." which is the unfailing sign of the amateur.

It's the artist's obligation to keep walking as close to the precipice as he can, and when he falls off (as he will, occasionally, unless he's cheating), he crawls back up and tries to find the edge of the precipice again.

To say it right isn't enough. You need to get them to listen, to understand, and finally to appreciate. If it is easy to read, amusing, and your audience knows a little more or is a little happier than before they read it, you have fulfilled the craft and art of writing.

The frightening reality is that no one is going to tap you on the shoulder and ask, "Are you a comedy writer?" So you must self-start, and even more difficult, finish. Then you stand up and say to the world, "Here's my work." Take your chances on the world saying, "This is the worst material I ever read in my whole life." It's just possible it won't. And what do they know, anyhow?

There is no security for the writer of humor. Anxiety goes with the territory. It's the cattle prod toward excellence. The artist without it is mediocre. The only writers I have seen succeed in avoiding it were the hacks—those who live by the timid truth, the self-serving lie, the superficial hypocrisy.

The top athlete, the successful tycoon, the heavyweight champion, the prima ballerina, the winner of the Pulitzer prize, all live with the fear of failure. Every champion has it, because without it you don't make champion. They know it takes only one unseen right cross, one fraction of a second in the race, one flat note, one false turn of a plot to send the adulatory crowd over to surround the new champion. The good ones know not only how difficult it is to be good, but how easy it is to miss.

From my own experience: I remember, after being an established writer for fifteen years, working on my own well-rated show, staring at the typewriter in the morning with that familiar gnawing still in the pit of my stomach—the fear that I couldn't do it, that I had been getting away with it all this time and I would at last be found out.

A top batting average in baseball is up around .333, which means that the player still failed about two out of three times. Shakespeare wrote some plays that are rarely, if ever, performed. The foremost sex object in the world has people who can't stand her, or him.

Financial independence, unassailable reputation, professional competence, all together aren't enough to assuage the fear that we might fall on our faces in front of everybody. And the good ones are most likely to have it. Because the pride they needed to get where they are is the same vulnerable pride that's endangered every time they go up to bat.

The most successful, those giving interviews in palatial suites at the Plaza Hotel, with agents outside the door waving six-figured contracts, with nubile companions of the sex of their choice in the next room, and the limousine waiting downstairs—they're scared, too. We all need to know that, so we don't castigate ourselves for our own insecurity, but learn to deal with it.

In the old days of live television, I remember the then young director, John Frankenheimer, after weeks of rehearsal, saying to his nervous cast just before air time, "Fuck them. Let's go do it." Anybody who performs—the pitcher in the world series, the rock and roll singer, the artist in the garret, the fighter before the fight—knows exactly what he meant.

They are your adversaries. They dare you to entertain them. Fuck them. If you fail, you go down the tubes. So if you succeed, make them pay. Make them buy you the Mercedes, beg for your autograph, thank you for your kindness, and make up for all past hurts. You've earned it.

And don't speak softly in front of their paper houses.

·8·

How to Work

*"The worst thing you write
is better than the
best thing you didn't write."*

What's the best way for a writer to work? Any way you can get it done. Thomas Wolfe wrote longhand on legal-size paper on the top of his refrigerator; Ring Lardner wrote in a tiny window-less room; some writers work best in a hot bath (mostly soft core romantic novels, I suspect); some need a phalanx of secretaries or machines to dictate to. (Personally, I am awed by any writer who needs shorthand or modern gadgets to keep up with the speed of his output.) Anyway, whatever works for you.

A bigger problem is how to start the creative output, how to get the words flowing, and how to keep at it. If you are one of those writers who sharpens pencils until (as Larry Gelbart puts it), they have an edge fine enough to use in brain surgery, and then finds indispensable errands such as replacing the battery for your quartz watch, try this modus operandi. It has worked not only for me, but for many other writers to whom I've recommended it.

The most energetic of us have at best three or four hours of good, creative productivity in a day. Find what time of day or night those hours are. Work those hours, only those hours and those same hours every day. (There's a danger in picking your best hours. Sometimes you feel so good you don't want to spoil it working.) I myself exclude weekends, legal and religious holidays, and commemorative holidays as remote as St. Swithin's Day, but that's optional.

What if you have a nine-to-five job, rear children, or have other responsibilities that restrict the options of your writing time? Within the available time, pick your best hours. It may be early in the morning, late at night, while the baby naps, while the others are watching television—whatever. An hour at a time, a block of hours on weekends, every evening, whatever works for you within your available hours and energy level. But strike a pattern. As closely as possible, the same hours at the same time. Make a schedule you can live with and stick to it. Make that time sacred. And make everyone around you hold it equally sacred. You will be surprised at how quickly both you and they will accept its sanctity.

During those hours you do not make or take telephone calls, you do not write letters, you do not straighten out your desk drawers. You do not check the box score of the ball game, or whether your cocktail gown was sent to the cleaners, or if the mail has come yet.

At the end of the time allotted, you put the cover on your typewriter and quit. Let me repeat that. At quitting time you quit. Even if you have not written a line. This is very important. It's as essential that you stop on schedule as that you start on time.

After you have stopped a few times with the first page still blank, you will be convinced that this writer is going to leave at quitting time, so it's best you get the work out of him before he goes. (The option that you could work later, or half the night if necessary, is not only depressing but encourages goofing off.)

Typewriter keys or pencil are not nearly as attractive to doodle with as are the paint and brush of the artist or the piano keys of a composer.

So.

If, after about an hour of writing time nothing is coming, start writing anyway. Write about the problems of the scene you're working on, write about what you would like in the scene, and perhaps even how another writer might write the scene if he didn't have your high standards. Or anything else, as long as it has to do with the project you're working on. Then, like the first batch of waffles, you throw away the first page.

The next morning, read over what you have written the day before. It gets the juices going again and is more likely to give you a running start than sharpening pencils or changing the typewriter ribbon.

So every day you sit in front of the typewriter for those appointed hours, or stand, or pace the floor. And eventually there's nothing else to do except write, unless . . .

Let's talk about writers' block. Writers' block is simply the fear that what you write will not be good enough. It probably won't, but write it anyway. It could be dreadful, but see, you don't have writers' block anymore.

The worst thing you write is better than the best thing you didn't write. All you wasted is some paper. (Use inexpensive second sheets by all means; there's nothing like pristine, twenty-pound bond paper to inhibit you from desecrating it with something inadequate). But before you crumple it up and make a two-point shot into the wastebasket, read it over. It just might have something of merit.

Let me, at this point, insert a method I sometimes use that may or may not be of help to anyone else. I'll describe it by first telling an anecdote. A miserly man learned that he could receive all the nourishment he needed from just inexpensive oatmeal and milk, so he ate it three times a day to save money. He finally got so sick of it he could no longer force it down. At that point he put a shot of bourbon on the table and promised himself that treat if he would just eat the bowl of oatmeal. With that in mind he was able to eat the oatmeal. After the final spoonful he poured the bourbon back into the bottle and said to himself, "Aha! That's the time I fooled you."

Sometimes, frustrated by the creative block, I would urge myself to at least put down the thoughts I already had, before I gave up. Just the notes, I would say to myself, so that I wouldn't forget them. And, so long as I was already putting them down, I might as well put them in the proper form. I would do so and, finally, the typewriter keys were clicking, I was finishing half-thoughts, putting words in their right order, moving on to other thoughts. . . .

"Aha!" I would think to myself, "that's the time I fooled you." It's possible that only my psyche is vulnerable to that kind of seducing, but it might be worth a try for you.

When the words won't come, don't press, don't quit, don't panic. Don't blame yourself for stupidity. Haven't you noticed how verbose stupid people are? Don't blame yourself for laziness. If you were really lazy, you would be an actor. Don't flay yourself with those masochistic self-doubts—what made me think I was a writer?—for that way lies frustration and agony.

Be kind to yourself.

Be as understanding of your frustrations as you would be if the struggling writer were your lover.

When a scene isn't working, when the writing isn't coming and the words don't flow, blame yourself last. Step back and examine it. It is usually because you don't have the proper ingredients, and almost always the missing ingredient is conflict.

Without conflict—unless you are writing a textbook—you have no life, no drive, no power train. People, in effusive praise of a performer, will sometimes say, "He could make a telephone book sound interesting." It's a big lie. One of my curses, when I'm fighting my own frustrations, is to see someone try. Conflict is what makes the wheels go around. It is even more important in humor than it is in drama.

I remember, on my first trip west in search of fame and fortune, sitting in the coach car munching a tasteless, overpriced cheese sandwich and fantasizing writing for Bob Hope. Supposing, for instance, I was assigned to write a scene where Bob Hope was registering for a room at a hotel.

From Kansas City to Albuquerque, I tried to write a humorous scene for a man who could make the phone book sound funny, and I couldn't think of even one mildly amusing line.

I broke into a sweat. I considered getting off at the water stop in Albuquerque and taking the next train back to Chicago. What made me think I was a comedy writer? If I couldn't think of even one funny line for a man registering in a hotel! Now if he were trying to sneak in a trained seal . . . or three other people at the same rate . . . or the hotel was filled and he'd have to double up with . . . or the room was so small that . . . or it was right next to. . . .

Anyway I stayed on the train. (Moral: Never forget the conflict and you may not have to go back to Chicago.)

I suppose that every practitioner of the creative arts is periodically asked the rather awed question, "Where do you get your ideas?" I never found a suitable answer—flip or serious—to what I considered a naive and unanswerable question. Until one day I heard myself asking the same naive, unanswerable question of a music composer.

And then, only a few years ago, sitting in on the early stages of rehearsal while actors improvised, I realized how I—and I presume most other practitioners of the creative arts—get ideas. We improvise. We improvise and keep improvising, changing and discarding until we get a usable line. We take that line and improvise on it, polishing and revising until, God willing, with persistence and luck, we may be left with a usable sequence—like the few grains of gold on the bottom of a mining pan.

And then, if that shiny stuff at the bottom of the pan assays out, and we can find someone in the marketplace who knows the genuine article when he sees it, we may be rewarded enough to buy a pair of boots and get drunk.

Artists, and storytellers especially, live in a world of "what if." We pick our character by the what if method. (What if he were a timid virgin . . .) We choose the situation. (What if he looked exactly like a member of the Mafia who was a womanizer . . .) I know I've what-ifed myself into a cliché, but that's the way improvising starts, and a good what-ifer improvises his way into something fresh and surprising.

I not only improvise, but I improvise dialogue aloud, which I would recommend to anyone writing words that must eventually be spoken. Often, especially when there are women or children in the scene, I end the day with badly strained vocal chords.

This improvisation could be, I believe, one of the most important reasons why writers of comedy often work in teams. It's difficult playing "let's pretend" by yourself. The other pervasive reason for writing in tandem is moral support in facing those two terrifying sights—the blank page and an unfeeling producer or editor.

Avoid talking about your work to anyone unless you have a definite purpose. I try to make it a rule, occasionally broken, never to expose my work except to a paying audience or a potential buyer. Be sure you are not showing it to people only because you need some strokes; they might not like it and you won't even get those. Talking about it dissipates the most powerful motivation for writing—the gratification of expression. Once you've talked about it, any further work is rewriting, which most writers will tell you is one of the more painful aspects of a frustrating profession.

It has been said that scripts aren't written, they're rewritten. You will usually find, after the frustration of the unwieldy, wordy first draft that didn't come out at all as you intended, that it is preferable to do the rewrite piecemeal rather than in one desperate lunge. To correct, with each pass, the more obvious errors. The work improves slowly, almost imperceptibly, until finally one day you have that surprised, heart-warming reaction, "Hey, that's not bad."

(I remember someone once offering Fred Allen a congratulatory, "Hey Fred, that show wasn't bad."

"It wasn't supposed to be," Fred Allen growled back.)

It goes without saying that the beginning writer, or the writer new to the media, should write consistently and continuously, with an assignment or not, to gain facility in the form. As long as you are writing anyway, you may as well write for a viable market. You get the practice, you're able to compare published or produced material with your own, and who knows, you may even sell it. It has happened. And, if it doesn't, you'll be a better writer than you were before you wrote it.

In the workshops I conduct, I try to find time to assign a "For the Hell of It" piece. This assignment is to write on any subject matter, of any length, any style, to ignore all market requirements, all do's and don'ts, all censorship. There is only one admonition—to write as entertainingly as possible

Because it was so writtten, with no inhibitions, no target or market, it is usually unsalable. For the same reason, it is almost always fresh, intriguing and well written. The finished product serves many purposes. It gives you the exhilaration of freedom, the pleasure of writing exactly what you wish, and the gratification of producing something good. Surprisingly, it is often closer to marketability than you expected.

The greatest value of this "For the Hell of It" piece, however, is in being an excellent sample of the writer's talent and craftsmanship. A number of writers have reported that, although they never sold it, this sample of their work was instrumental in getting other assignments.

One of the most useful self-help devices for the writer—better than lectures, better than this or any other book—is a writers' workshop. It provides a stimulating environment for the best possible training for a writer, which is writing.

I have conducted workshops with almost always positive and encouraging results. Occasionally, when I had to discontinue one because of other responsibilities, I was pleased to find the writers continued the workshop, conductorless, for the support and productivity it offered.

Writing is one of the loneliest of professions. The writers' workshop, like the art class, provides not only camaraderie and friendly counsel, but also an incentive toward bringing something in for show and tell.

But wasn't there, in this very same chapter, an admonition against showing or talking about your work? Two explanations for that seeming contradiction: First, talking about it after a draft and *during* the process, for constructive discussion, is often useful. Second, if consistency were one of my strong points, this book would be on how to operate a paint store.

·9·

"Cut, Cut, Cut"

*"I wanted to write you
a short letter
but I don't have the time,
so I'll have to write
a long one."*

Cut, cut, cut.

If you are able to cut four pages to two without losing the essentials, you have made it twice as good. Avoid embellishments, like the old-fashioned, distracting curlicues we once thought made beautiful handwriting. No sideshows, no, "Look ma, I'm dancing" showing off. Every line should build character, build interest, build suspense, move toward your goal, or be ruthlessly blue-penciled.

If you are telling a funny incident about how you had hit a police car and your bumpers got locked, we don't have to know that you were on your way to your accountant. And when the story's over, don't make them hang around while you wave goodbye to the friendly natives. Take your bow, leave them laughing, and anytime you want to come back you'll be more than welcome.

Notice the way a good ball player moves after a ball, a fighter throws a punch, an expert tennis player swings a racket—without wasted motion. This not only gives them grace and saves energy, but allows them to concentrate all thoughts and efforts on only the necessary steps to the immediate goal. A blue pencil—cutting out unnecessary words, phrases, or sentences—is one of the most valuable tools for the comedy writer. Take the age-old joke (perhaps the first one since the recorded history of jokes), "Why does a chicken cross the road?" Punch line: "To get to the other side." Possibly, even probably, that line was first written something like, "Because it wants to get to the other side." Take away the first three words and notice how much sharper, simpler, clearer, and *funnier* the joke becomes.

It has been said that the mark of a fine comedy writer is one who can cut out a line he thinks is the best in his work, a standard I haven't always been able to achieve. I do remember once, however, finding I had to cut a minute and a half from a script I thought was already cut to the bone. I excised a joke here, a phrase there, even getting down to cutting single words until, tortuously, I got it down to the required length and turned it in with much moaning about how I had been forced to desecrate my script. I was then informed that, because of a readjustment, there would be another minute available which I could use to replace some of my precious words. I studied the castoff material and could find not one word, phrase, or sentence I wanted to put back.

So . . . say what you have to say in as few words as possible.

And get off.

Like this.

·10·

The Marketplace

*"Television, the cinema, the stage,
night clubs, the after-dinner speech,
articles, books, cartoons,
advertising, greeting cards—
pick a category.
Anyone can apply."*

"There's nothing obscene about making money," said George Bernard Shaw. And further documentation from an equally distinguished writer, Samuel Johnson, as quoted in *Writer's Market* of 1944 *and* 1984, who said, "Any man who writes, and does not write for money, is a plain damn fool."

Of all the major nominees at award shows, the writer is usually the only one who shows up in a rented tux. There is the artist fortunate enough to be commercially successful, and there is the artist gifted enough to touch people. But the artist who does both is rare and blessed. On the other hand, the talented writer who *patronizingly* stoops to writing for money usually fails. It's the lesser talent, doing his best, who makes it.

Don't trust a writer who cares nothing for money. On the other hand, no respect is due the writer who cares only for money. The first belongs in an ivory tower, the second in a box factory.

Hindi Brooks, now a successful television writer, was a schoolteacher when she came into my writer's workshop years ago. At that time her avocation was writing clever, noncommercial skits and playlets. While doing research for this chapter, I asked her what, from the workshop, was most instrumental in her successful transition to the professional field. "The most important thing I learned in that workshop," she answered, "was, 'If you get enough gratification writing this cute, clever stuff for your friends, great. It's a wonderful hobby. But if you want to make a living at it, get out into the marketplace, find out what they're buying, and do your best to deliver it to them.' "

That's what this chapter's all about. To those not interested in the compensation of writing: skip this chapter, do not pass Go, do not collect $200. To those who wish to get paid for their craft: get out into the marketplace, find out what they're buying, and do your best to deliver it to them.

Let's start with what might belong in a chapter you won't find in this book, "How to *Avoid* Making Money As a Writer." If I were writing such a chapter, I'd begin with poetry. (I had a publisher tell me he'd rather find a burglar in his office than a poet.) Next, I'd list short stories and one-act plays. I can hear the cries of anguish—some of them my own. The short story and one-act play are two of my favorite forms, both as a writer and reader. They are typically American in style, temperament, and brevity. But they are not "commercial," which means that although they may win awards and reprints in anthologies, they won't make the car payments or buy the obligatory designer jeans for a daughter in junior high. If you insist on writing them, my blessings and respect. I would read them, but I don't know many others who will, and too few will buy them.

The active comedy market today, where substantial sums of money might change hands, are comic strips, books, articles, material for stand-up comedians, the theater, motion pictures, and television.

Supplying material—often free-lance—for comedians has been a stepping-stone for many writers of humor, including some of the most successful: Neil Simon, Woody Allen, Mel Brooks, Dick Cavett, to name a few. The usual way to enter this market is to send established comedians or their agents an inventory of custom-written jokes. If they are interested—and some of the most famous are, more often than you would expect—they will ask for more, choose the jokes they like and pay piecework.

Writing to comedians in care of the theater, nightclub, or TV channel from which they are performing (if no more precise address is available), with a frank statement of your purpose, will usually get a response from at least some of their agents. They need you, too.

Writing jokes for public speakers follows the same techniques as writing for the stand-up comic, except the former is more personal and tailored to a specific place and audience. Assignments in this field are gained by reputation, coincidence, catch-as-catch-can, or all three.

Jokes are also used, in adapted forms, in cartoons, greeting cards, and even advertising copy. The writers in these fields, whose primary focus may not always be comedy, still find humor a valuable additional tool.

Much of the best-written humor in America today is in cartoons and comic strips. It is generally far wittier than television or motion picture comedy, and almost always more sophisticated. This is ironic, since it started out as, and was until comparatively recently, an elementary form of humor for children. It is probably because comic strips are relatively uncorrupted and go almost directly from the creator to the audience, with just an editor between, who only seldom has the authority and almost never the inclination to interfere.

Writing gags for free-lance cartoonists is both a demanding and competitive market. The gag lines had better be topical, original, brief, simple, and funny in this buyer's market. They are usually submitted ten to twenty at a time on 3x5 file cards. The annual *Writer's Market* has a listing of these markets, accompanied by descriptions of their specific needs.

Greeting cards make profuse and sometimes profane use of humor. A survey of this market showed very little consensus, except that submissions be brief, simple, and upwards of 90 percent of the time, directed toward women purchasers. (Men, it seems, rarely buy greeting cards, a provocative fact that belongs in another book entirely.)

Good news for those of us in the comedy field is that almost all were interested in humor. In answer to a questionnaire, most greeting card publishers found comedy an important selling asset and welcomed submissions. Not as many, but still a good percentage, announced themselves in the market for risqué messages, from the subtle to the brazenly overt. With few exceptions, most demanded topical subject material. In regards to comedy in greeting cards, here are the qualities most frequently requested: "contemporary" . . . "don't be subtle" . . . "short" . . . "easy to understand" . . . "puns" . . . "mix sex with humor" . . . "drop dead funny" . . . "outrageous" . . . "funny enough to knock us off our feet" . . . "something that makes us laugh at the absurdities and realities of life". . . .

As is apparent, these are desirable qualities for all humor, with two notable exceptions. Greeting cards are usually non-controversial and are always tailored to a specific audience for a specific purpose.

The fees for accepted ideas range roughly from $10 to $75 with, in a few cases, the payment of royalties. *Writer's Market* contains a comprehensive list of greeting-card publishers with essential information on specific needs, taboos, and tips.

Gags for both cartoons and greeting-card messages offer little more than a minimum livelihood. But they are markets that are always active, open to almost anyone, and can help keep food on the table until you accumulate the expertise and credentials to set up shop in more profitable and promising areas.

Humor in advertising copy is one of the most difficult kinds to write. You must make them laugh while you are trying to sell them something, and all in a minuscule amount of space or time. The second most important purpose is to make them laugh; the first is the sale. That's why it is almost always done by copywriters with a flair for comedy, rather than comedy writers with an aptitude for advertising.

Since the advertiser has ceased being so uptight about his product, there has been more (welcome) humor in advertising copy. There was a time when television sponsors thought of the painstakingly written scenes we sweated over as filler between their commercials.

It is well to remember that, although advertisers are now usually loose enough to allow jokes about almost anything or anybody, the product itself is still sacrosanct. Some more sacrosanct than others. You rarely see humor in ads about perfume or cosmetics. You rarely see ads about beer done seriously. Yet many people, including myself and Omar Khayyam, think the second more important in the scheme of things.

Since humor in advertising copy is almost always done by professional copywriters, the market is almost exclusively in advertising agencies with staff people. It is rarely, if ever, freelance. Employment is attained by applying to the agencies themselves.

Comedy articles in print are probably closest to the purest form; going *almost* directly from manufacturer to consumer in a straight line untouched by human hands. No kibitzers and no ambushers lying in wait. (So what do we usually do when we attain this freedom? Take our smudged pages in our sweaty hands and beg *anybody* to give us their opinion. But this is a book on writing, not psychology.)

The humorous article or column is a modern version of the essay, my first love. Like any first love, it still seems the most desirable. But perhaps that's only in the retrospect of dreams and nostalgia. Three of the best in the field are Art Buchwald, Russell Baker, and Erma Bombeck. I'm quite certain that they, and the others, would tell us that the syndicated comedy column is unteachable, and recommend that candidates for the field have the skin of a rhinoceros, the endurance of a marathon runner, and a wealthy spouse.

The humorous article is almost entirely anecdotal observation. But that, in fact, is a substantial and significant part of all comedy. The comedy article is also usually more personal than the serious piece.

You start by taking a familiar annoyance, problem, embarrassment, or misfortune, then standing back to look at it in perspective. Everything is more tolerable *and* funnier when looked at in perspective. (Remember the well-meaning friend trying to cheer you up with the annoying, "Someday you'll laugh at all this"? Yes, but if you could just go to your friendly comedy writer you wouldn't have to wait so long.)

Then you compound the misfortune . . . "We waited two hours at the wrong bus stop . . ." "He said it would take three

days and cost $50, and it came in six months with a bill for $750
..." Don't worry about making it too long or too much. It's not
happening to your audience who, in this version, are the only
ones who really count.

These kinds of stories don't need a "happy" ending, in
fact they usually end with the biggest misfortune of all, because
it's happening to somebody else. ("Minor surgery," someone—I'd bet it wasn't a doctor—once said, "is surgery that
happens to someone else.") Good comedy is not cruel, because
it's happening in perspective. If the person is actually feeling
pain it's not good comedy, it's not funny, it's not even healthy.

Full-length books of humor, as full-length motion pictures
and plays, are the most difficult to write. (And, if unsuccessful,
the most difficult to read.) They require an inordinate amount
of concentration, which is a requisite of any creative art, over
an inordinate amount of time for both writer and audience.

There have been some fine writers of the genre, all the way
from the classic Boccaccio, Dickens, Twain, et al, to the modern day S.J. Perelman, James Thurber, Erma Bombeck, Russell
Baker (I omit collections of articles). But almost all of those humorists had the temerity to write full-length, and the gratification of being read, because they had already gained a reputation
and following in the shorter forms.

The construction of the humorous book is the same as all
humor—and drama—with this exception: books need subject
matter, characters *and* conflict with the endurance to remain viable through at least 200 pages, rather than just two lines or one
scene.

So you pick interesting likeable characters and put them
into an intriguing situation. Just as you would with a story or
joke. Except that this time you had better choose very carefully.
Because you have to be there with them for months and months,
and your reader has to want to be there for pages and pages.

Nonbooks, as the minisized, humorous paperbacks on a

single subject are called by publishers (*Real Men Don't Eat Quiche* and *How to Be a Jewish Mother* are examples) have a life all their own. They are made up of gags in the original sense of the word, all sharing, as was pointed out in Chapter 3, the same first act. That first act in this form, however, is especially crucial. It must be intriguingly provocative and have the capacity to breed many punch lines. Since it is also the title, it should be as compelling as a top sergeant and as seductive as a hot fudge sundae. No one is going to buy the book for plot or information.

Once you get that all-important line, it needs only freshness and wit. No wrestling with plot construction, motivation, character development, or suspense. That's why it's called a nonbook. Comedy writers, when they create or are given such a line, find it as irresistible as an open jar of peanuts on the coffee table. I have seen writers (let's be candid, I have been one of those writers) who will ignore their own assignment and "pitch" on an innocuous line of this sort, like children playing games instead of doing their homework.

Anyone familiar with the lengths to which the professional writer will usually go to avoid plying his trade won't be surprised at this phenomenon. My own explanation is that it's a quick and gratifying "fix" in the ofttimes frustrating tedium of writing. Plus the fact that anything that doesn't have pressure isn't really work.

The fundamentals of humor are the same all the way from the face-making of a four-year-old to the suave witticisms of Noel Coward. Two things, however, set apart the stage play, or the legitimate theater, as it is called (probably for the patronizing reason that it considers all other forms of live entertainment bastardizations) from other media: the physical proximity to the audience, and the cost—especially when compared to motion pictures or television—to attend. It takes something quite unusual and compelling to motivate a person to get tickets in advance, tolerate the narrow seats, and brave too-hot-in-summer and too-cold-in-winter theaters. Once you get them in, however, they will stay at least until the intermission and—like eating the rice pudding because it comes with the dinner—will usually stay until the bitter end.

So the writer does not have to keep them riveted in their seats because they do not go out for popcorn as in the movies, or have the unremitting competition of other channels as in television, where they don't even have to get out of their chair, for godsakes. (Ever notice how impotent a television watcher feels when his remote control unit is out of reach?)

On Broadway, the splashy, expensive musical, directed mostly to expense-account buyers and tourists, seems to have taken over. (Although lately, probably because it has grown top heavy with production costs, it seems, perhaps temporarily, to have come upon hard times, also.) The nonmusical plays are usually imports, regional theater, or off-Broadway. Of those, only a small proportion are comedy, a reversal of the trend a generation ago.

However, this rather bleak picture is brightened considerably by the burgeoning regional theater, which is more accessible to the new writer than Broadway ever was. These markets are comparatively easy to find and reach. Most are receptive to original material.

Another encouraging characteristic of these vital theater groups is that a stage reading by competent actors is not only available but usually encouraged. Most writers agree that hearing the words aloud will tell them more about a scene than hours and days of perusing the script.

Then there is the gratification of a live audience. I remember the euphoric feeling of standing in the back of the theater and hearing real live people who had paid real money, laughing at my lines. It was my first stage production, so when I found that I was not only expected but welcomed at any performance, I returned at every opportunity, soaking up the audience reaction like a moisture-parched plant in a welcome shower. What a contrast to television and motion pictures where, once in production, a writer was usually considered a hindrance.

There was one line intended merely as a cover to the necessary wait as a character crossed the stage to open the door. "Did you ever notice," another character said, while searching the bar for some Scotch, "that no matter how much drinking goes on in a house, there's always tequila left?"

To my surprise, and probably yours, the line was greeted with a substantial laugh every night. I had, of course, hit upon that most responsive chord of identification; but I would never have known it if I had not been right there with flesh-and-blood people hearing it for the first time.

The writer's powerful contractual position in the theater (no line in the script can be changed without his consent—a writer's dream) should make a bigger difference than it does. In practice, the threat of the producer canceling production, or an actor walking out if thwarted in requested script changes, dilutes much of the writer's control.

The ingenuity required to keep the action within the physical confines of a stage usually more than balances its disadvantages. Most stage productions adapted to the screen, despite the many more production opportunities, are not improved by the transition.

Now let's go to the movies. Scripts here are usually adaptations of successes in other mediums, or assignments, or originals by writers with impressive credits. For the outsider, the studios no longer offer a very good prospect for a script sale.

The studios have departments to which they will refer you for submissions. They almost always require that you sign a waiver and often stipulate that you submit through an accredited agent.

Most of the projects are brought in from the outside and developed in tandem with independent producers. These independent producers are good contacts for the writer of an original script. Possibly an even better approach is to interest a bankable star or director.

There isn't any tried and true method for reaching these people, outside of chance or a good agent. An agent who is interested in your work, has good judgment and contacts, and is willing to extend effort on your behalf. A rare parley. If you can make it I'd like to be with you on your next visit to the race track. (More on agents in Chapters 11 and 12.)

I have never worked in public television, but I think it needs at least a comment in this chapter. It is a medium for which I have a combination of respect and sympathy. (A friend, some time ago, described his impression of public television as erudite people talking about things he felt guilty for not listening to.) Fortunately, that general impression is now changing.

Public TV has fine dramas to its credit (although, unhappily, they too often seem to be imported from England). The artists are often more talented and paid less than those in commercial television, which is usually accepted as the way it should be. (A curious and common attitude seems to be that artists are expected to accept less compensation for the opportunity to do quality work.) However, this is a medium which doesn't, as a rule, offer assignments directly to the comedy writer.

So we come to television comedy.

Television humor is in a sorry state at the moment. This is especially depressing to those of us who started way back in the pretelevision days ("Duffy's Tavern," "Fred Allen," "Burns and Allen," "Jack Benny"), who came through what now seem the golden days of television comedy ("Your Show of Shows," "Mr. Peepers," "Jackie Gleason," "I Love Lucy"), up through the relatively modern era ("All in the Family," "M*A*S*H," and "Soap") and now dwindling down to a precious few with such as "Cheers" and "The Bill Cosby Show."

The depressingly few good situation comedies, and the occasional new comedian on talk shows, are about the only quality comedy we have in television. I believe this is because in this medium there are too many noncreative people who make creative contributions, temporary help who make permanent decisions, and nervous underlings who make dangerous moves. It's not that they're unintelligent—they're just scared and uninspired.

On my first well-paying job, I confided to a veteran writer that I felt overpaid, since I would have gladly worked at my chosen profession for less. "Don't say that," he said angrily, "don't ever say that. Always remember that only one-third of what they pay you is for what you do. The other two-thirds are for what they do to you."

But despite all the above, I would suggest that comedy writers starting today give strong consideration to the field of television. That's where the action is, that's where the money is, and that's where the opportunities are. It's one of the few games in town. But only if your bent lies in that direction. Then do the best you can, go as far as you can, be as original as you can. And even if you don't get to be another Norman Lear, you may perhaps be able to bring up the standards ever so slightly, make it better for those who come after you, and more gratifying for those of us who have been there before.

But that needs a chapter all by itself. . . .

·11·

Selling

*"Go for rich and famous,
and don't settle for
less than one."*

Let's talk about how to get a foothold in the active, profitable, voracious market of television comedy. By far the largest (and usually best-paying) user of material in that market is the so-called situation comedy. Often referred to as sit-com (a contraction I dislike) the more accurate description is, even in the poorest of the form, character comedy. There are not nearly enough even improbable and barely possible situations to satisfy that insatiable appetite. Take it from those of us who have tried. It is, in its best form, *interesting characters' reactions to normal situations*. (As opposed to soap operas, where exotic characters are put into unusual situations.)

Start by picking a show you like. You will write best what you like best, and you will be paid best for what you do best. If you don't like any of them, you have a problem. You are in the predicament of a pastry chef who hates desserts. You don't know whether your product is bad until it's too late. If the show isn't as good as you like, don't worry about that. Maybe you can make it better.

Watch the show consistently. Ignore those snobs who declare they never watch television. That's a luxury that those who hope to make a career in this field can't afford. (There is snob appeal in disdaining anything that's popular. This was the same breed whose claim to superiority, before television, was never listening to radio, never watching domestically made movies, and before that, disdaining novels because they were superficial, way back to Sophocles, whose plays they didn't see because they were too frivolous.)

That a man, at an exhibit of Picasso, turns to look at a pretty girl with skirts flying in the breeze, or a woman watching a lovely sunset turns around when someone says, "There goes Tom Selleck," that someone would rather listen to gossip about a neighbor than a concert by Brahms, doesn't mean they have no taste. It only indicates the variety of appetites, some of which—immediate and fleeting—are not framed and hanging, so people must look when they can.

Eating hot dogs at a ball game, or cold cuts while playing

poker, or beer between turns at bowling, doesn't necessarily mean one is not a gourmet. Rather, perhaps, that one has choices, and is saving the Veal Oscar and vintage wine for the more appropriate environment and the leisure time to enjoy it to the fullest.

Dickens, Shakespeare, Mark Twain, Poe are but a few of those who wrote unabashedly for entertainment, and never accepted the rigid reverence demanded by those who would be our cultural dictators. The true measure of the writer of entertainment is the same as that of any craftsman—that he do his job with competence and integrity. Nothing more or less.

The Writers Guild of America periodically lists, in its newsletter, series that are in production, which shows are open for assignments, which operate only through agents, names of essential contacts—production companies, producers, leading actors, and directors. The Writers Guild Newsletter is available to nonmembers at $2.50 a copy or $20 a year (it publishes once a month, excluding July and August). The mailing address is: Writers Guild of America West, 8955 Beverly Blvd., Los Angeles, CA 90048, % Newsletter.

The *Daily Variety* and *Hollywood Reporter* have end-of-the-week production charts, also with a listing of personnel and other information. (I'm not assuming you don't have an agent, just that even if you do have one, you need something to do while you're waiting for him to call.) Contact whomever you can by whatever method you can.

Assuming you have made contact and have been invited to submit, let's go on to the next step. If you can, get samples of what they consider their better episodes. (The M.B.A., Minimum Basic Agreement, of the Writers Guild has certain restrictions against what is considered "speculative" writing—usually concerning established writers. Therefore, the following presumes that those conditions are complied with.)

Let's deal with the actual submission of a story line, treatment, or script. The following recommendations apply to scripts for a series, pilots for proposed series, TV movies of the week, as well as theatrical motion picture scripts.

A shooting script, however, is a story written to be seen, not read. Therefore, it is difficult—sometimes even tedious—to read, analyze, and judge, even for the most perceptive of producers. Not to mention the producer who *never* reads (whether because of inclination or inability is not disclosed). Almost always, unless the decision for production has already been made, producers would prefer to first see a treatment.

It goes without saying that you always write with your audience in mind. It needs saying, however, that often you have to write first—especially in the case of screen, television, or stage scripts—for an audience of one. The one who will decide whether it gets made. One who usually hasn't the patience, hasn't the time, and too often hasn't the ability to judge a script that was written to be performed rather than read. But before you can get to the real audience in the real world, you must get past the producer. The dragon at the castle gate guarding the beautiful virgin is less forbidding, and might have better taste.

So.

If you want in that castle, if you want to bring that virgin home to meet your mother, you must first get past the dragon. (Unless you have clout enough to get your work performed anyway—in which case you can skip this chapter.)

A treatment is used to show plot, characters, and scenes of the story to be told. It is always written before the script is, and can have one of two different purposes. One is so that the people involved in the scheduled production may see what shortcomings there might be, what possible problems may come up, and what additions or changes need to be made. The other purpose is to serve as a presentation to interest the powers-that-be in doing the project. It is the latter reason we are concerned with here.

Most experienced writers have found that putting a few

jokes in the presentation—witticisms that may never appear in the final version—adds immeasurably to the project's chances. (Careful, though, a bad joke can ruin everything.) Once you're past the glabrous dragon you can redirect your aim toward real people, while this one's busy breathing fire on other quivering ink-stained souls.

When you have access to the producer, it's best to keep in mind that at this time she is primarily, and probably solely, interested in the story. If the name on the script or treatment is accompanied by a reputation, writing competence is taken for granted. If you are unknown, she is only interested if you have a new and intriguing story. (At this stage, quality may have nothing to do with acceptance or rejection. Of first importance here is whether it is the *kind* of story she is looking for, and not too similar to something that has already been done.)

You must still, even though you have an audience of only one, present it as beguilingly, concisely, and clearly as you can. Otherwise, she may be the biggest audience you'll ever get for the project. Give indications, by jokes or graphic scenes, how intriguing and funny your story is. (Don't, under any circumstances, fall victim to the amateur's vague promise, ". . .and a lot of very funny things happen right here.")

If you have a choice—and don't live 2000 miles away—present your story orally unless you have psychological inhibitions or severe speech impediments. It is more effective, if also more nerve-racking. Too many deficiencies in your story-telling can be harmful, however. Keep in mind that you are giving a performance. I would rehearse, as an actor does, with the same meticulous care. It is important to tell your story smoothly, with no pauses, stumbling, stuttering, or word searching, and no omission of crucial story points.

Another mark of the amateur is to shoot at the producer, with almost machine-gun speed, one story line after another, with a "take your pick" attitude. It is the abdication of your responsibility of choice, which the producer has neither the inclination, time, nor aptitude to take over. Come in with your best effort. I do recommend having at least one spare story line in reserve in case you are stopped in the first thirty seconds, as often happens, by "We've done that" or "We don't do that kind of story." In that case, so that the sought-after conference may not be aborted, you have the reserve story to throw into the breach. In any case, just as in showing jewelry, it diminishes the effect to display more than one piece at a time.

It is best also to have a written version of the project with you, to leave with the producer in case he is interested. I am not saying that all producers have a short attention span or memory, but it's better not to take that chance.

For those who live too far away for the personal interview, the presentation can be submitted—with or without an agent— by mail. Eventually, however, if there is enough interest in the project, a personally attended meeting is very important, if not a necessity. You and your correspondent will be the best judge of when that time will be.

If all this sounds perilously close to huckstering, that's because it is. First and foremost is competence at the craft. But if you can also present it persuasively. . . .

Just as there are catch phrases in selling cars (low mileage, smooth ride, fast starting) there are certain desirable buzz words in speaking of a script—*relevance* and *warmth,* for instance. Experienced writers drop them into story conferences whenever they can. Like a breast-pocket handkerchief, even if they don't serve a useful purpose, they make a nice impression.

(Something that reinforces this point happened once when I was called to New York to doctor a series in trouble. I was met at the plane by friends and we spent the better part of the night at a convenient watering hole catching up on news. I arrived at the luncheon conference the next day with a hangover of heroic proportions. Immediately, a crab salad was put in front of me and I felt a wave of nausea. The others discussed the show problems while I kept my head down trying to keep my stomach steady. Finally, aware of my role as the Lochinvar from out of the west, at a pause in the conversation I lifted my head and said, "What this show needs is more warmth." My own words almost did me in. I put my eyes down and didn't dare speak another word for the rest of the meal. Then I hurried to an open window and drew in deep gulps of fresh air. I felt a hand on my shoulder and a voice, (to this day I don't know who it was) saying, "Mr. (the sponsor) likes you," the voice said. "He just told me. He said, 'That writer doesn't talk much, but when he says something. . . .' "

Let's assume you've passed the first stage and they want you to submit a script. Or that you're geographically located where it would be impractical if not impossible to arrange a personal interview. It's time to address a mundane and pragmatic subject that has little to do with either art or craft—the physical look and format of the script or treatment.

We'll start first with the most elementary of admonitions—neatness counts. It counts like hell. A clean script in the proper form is the sign of a professional. We write carefully to create an emotion, hold interest, gain momentum, and come to a resounding climax. And we can lose one or all of these elements in the most carefully executed scene by a blemished erasure, a transposed letter, or misspelled word. These are distractions, sometimes fatal, to the reader interest we are counting on. Notice that when a comedian stumbles over a word he will not finish the joke. He knows it is hopeless. He has lost the concentration he needs from you to make it pay off.

If another reason is necessary, here it is. There is something about the pristine look of a clean, unblemished page that inhibits the itchy pencil of the compulsive rewriter. Once you have admitted, by a crossed out or changed word, that you have suffered some doubts, he feels free to show you others. And seeing a producer pick up a blue pencil while reading your script is akin to the feeling you get in the examination room when you see the doctor putting on one rubber glove.

Another point. Remember your mother's warning. Who

knows but that on your way to the producer's office you may get into an accident and have to go in with a soiled script.

Script formats vary from studio to studio and producer to producer, but they are all basically the same. Following certain general rules will make a script adaptable to the different requirements. (The script in Chapter 16 generally conforms to most formats. It differs from the writer's script only in that every camera setup and the position of the camera has been identified and numbered.)

Camera angles, set descriptions, sound and music directions are usually in capital letters to set them off from dialogue. It is a common mistake for the writer to put in too many camera shots, such as close-ups, long, medium, over-the-shoulder shots. The director will make his own decisions, as he should, and camera shots only clutter up the script. (Many directors admit to ignoring writer directions entirely.) Exceptions, of course, are when the camera direction is vital to a story point.

There's also a prevalent temptation for writers to give too many, too detailed line interpretations to the performer. Again, excepting those times that the desirable reaction is not obvious in the dialogue, assume the actor is competent and give him the leeway to at least try his own interpretation. (Just as he must assume that you know what you are doing and trust your intelligence, if not the infallibility of your judgment.) The ideal situation is, of course, when all three—writer, director, actor—have the same general goal, mutual faith in each others' competence, and the assurance that this confidence will outweigh the respective egos. It's beautiful when you get it, still workable when you have two out of three, but if it's only one out of three that's when the aluminum siding business you left begins to look good to you.

Keeping the script clear of all but the necessary directions has a further advantage. Scripts are written to be performed, not to be read, and one cluttered with directions such as "medium shot . . . over-the-shoulder-shot . . . she looks at him musingly

. . . capriciously . . ." only tend to make it more difficult to follow.

My procedure, for which I don't remember ever receiving any complaints, is giving only the master shot, one full camera angle encompassing the entire set and characters, at the beginning of a scene.

JONES LIVING ROOM. NIGHT
Joe and Ed are present.

No other direction except an essential costume, demeanor, prop, or lighting specification that the director might not be aware of. No stage crosses, no bust shots, no "looks idly out of the window," unless, again, they are necessary to the story and not obvious to the actor and director.

How long should the script be? Comedy scripts, because of the expected response of laughter—either live or canned— are usually shorter than dramatic scripts. The net time on a half-hour television show, subtracting commercial and station announcements, is approximately twenty-four and a half minutes. The script will be twenty-eight to thirty-two pages long. A sixty-minute show is, of course, twice that. The two-hour teleplay, or movie of the week as it's usually called, runs about 100 pages, and the full-length feature screenplay about 120.

Most producers like overlong scripts. I don't. They prefer them because it gives them many options of what to cut. I don't like them for exactly the same reason. Although cutting a script is difficult, and the temptation to let someone else shoulder the work and responsibility very strong, the writer is most often the best qualified to do it. I tend, as the majority of writers do, to write long. And, although many producers and directors can be of inestimable value in cutting a script, some are unaware of what the necessary linchpins in a script are, the essential plot lines, and those lines and passages that will be missed least.

A treatment or outline can be almost any length. When it

serves as the blueprint of the script—which is usually on assignment—it may be as long as sixty pages.(I remember one instance when it was longer than the script.) Or it may be as short as one-half page. It is up to the writer to tell only what he feels will "sell" the story and no more. (Remember the admonition of not overestimating the attention span of executives?)

I must admit that I am not always unprejudiced in the writer-producer relationship. I try, God knows I try. But I think it's time to hear it for the producers. First let's read them their Miranda rights.

It's their ball, their final responsibility, often their money. Producers are people. (Now you can't be more fair than *that*.) They are intelligent, not so intelligent, creative, noncreative, egocentric, and self-effacing, with integrity ranging all the way from a great deal to very little. Just like any civilian. Just like you.

And, assuming that both you and the producer have all the above attributes on the positive side, there will still be honest differences over honest issues. It behooves you to be neither cowardly nor stupidly stubborn. Make your point. Then, if you have to, give way on uncritical points, negotiate the important ones, and try not to compromise on principles. There is no telling you when to fight and when to run. You back and file, and stand firm, and give way; it's hoped the qualified producer will do the same.

So, what is, as they say, the bottom line?

Prepare as best you can, go out with the tide, and pray for a fair wind.

I suppose that any book about professional writing should have a section about agents. I know little about agents (an admission I don't mind making), except that they are important (especially in the field of television and feature pictures), as witness the fact that many of the studios are headed by reformed agents.

Perhaps this doesn't need saying, but I don't want to take that chance: a legitimate agent, in my experience, never asks for a fee in advance, and unless there are other services involved, doesn't take more than 10 percent of your fee.

Another cautionary note: an agent, for one of many reasons, even though he's honest and competent, may value the goodwill of the studio, producer, or publisher with whom he is negotiating over that of his own client.

Also, although a percentage of your fee may sound like an equitable and adequate incentive to his making the best deal for you, there are elements—credit, working conditions, secretary, the all-important location of your parking space, that may be very important to you but of no remunerative value to him. (Some of them are already resentful because they feel you're getting 90 percent of *their* money.)

This part of negotiations may be protected by a lawyer in lieu of or in addition to your other representation. I would not put a lawyer any higher than an agent on my all-time list of true-blue, unselfish representatives, but at least he has no vested interest in the goodwill of your employer. (A fellow writer, planning to move to the west coast, made an exploratory trip first to assemble what he called the three essentials to a writer: a therapist, an agent, and a lawyer. He made a one-stop solution instead—he got married. Which worked for about five years, after which he needed the above triumvirate plus *two* lawyers.)

So.

We get back to the oft-repeated exhortation—learn your craft. A by-product benefit is that you won't be so dependent on that man in the cashmere sport coat who doesn't return your calls.

·12·

Most Frequently Asked Questions

"You in the back there,
with your hand up."

Any professional writer will tell you that most of the questions asked by new writers are the same. Following are some of those most frequently asked. Many have already been answered in detail elsewhere, so they will be dealt with only briefly here.

How do I get my start?

Learn your craft.

Knock at every door.

Seek out and explore every possible market. Design your product to fit that market. If it doesn't, redesign it or find another market.

Keep learning and keep knocking.

How do I get my material read by the potential buyer?

Consult *Writer's Market,* the Writers Guild market letter, production schedules in the trade papers such as *Variety* and *Hollywood Reporter,* and any other market listing you can find.

Find the specific person who represents the specific market for that material. For ongoing series it is usually the producer; for new material to production companies or studios, the department of program development. Write or call to find whether that market is open and, as exactly as possible, what their needs are.

Convince them that you are professional and competent.

Get an agent. (See next question.)

How do I get an agent?

Any way you can.

The easiest way is to become a success first. The second easiest way is nonexistent. As a matter of fact, there is only one other way. To find one who is interested in your work and feels he can make money with it.

Getting an agent is like a bank loan. The best way to get one is to prove you don't need it.

An imposing problem—especially to neophyte writers—is

that some publishers, and a large proportion of studios and producers, will consider submissions only through agents. I have been told that this is to avoid lawsuits. Another reason is that they are trying to save the time and bother of screening out the incompetent and frivolous. The agent, in turn, to save himself time and bother, usually screens out all unknowns. (Another Catch Twenty-Two. As you go along you will find in this profession the Catches go way past that number.)

But let's try to be positive. There are some producers who will consider unrepresented work and there are agents who will represent an unknown. Find one and, with an impressive sample of work and some luck, after a while the others will come looking for you.

Is it better to work with a big agency or a small one?

The question is immaterial. The best agent for the not-yet-established writer is the one with most confidence in your ability. Again there is no second best. The agent who has no confidence in your ability will leave your work unread, your calls unanswered, and your name unspoken.

How do I know it's funny?

You don't, for sure, until it's passed the three vital tests. The first and most important is if it's funny to you. If you think so, then it is, until you're proven wrong. The second is if it's funny to the one who will use it. (If he rejects it, that doesn't prove it isn't funny, but without that middle man or woman, you will never know for sure.) The final and indisputable test is by the audience. Assuming your material is competently presented, it's funny if they think it's funny and if they don't—back to the typewriter.

A note of caution. If you don't think it's funny, forget it, no matter how many people laugh. Using comedy lines that you yourself don't react to is like having a teetotaler choose the dinner wine.

How do I keep my material from being stolen?

First, don't worry too much about it. To sell your product, you need exposure, and it would be counterproductive to keep it under wraps. Supermarkets expect a certain percentage of shoplifting, but take the risk in order to make the products easily available.

Most legitimate buyers in the marketplace feel fortunate enough just to find usable material. At their customary fees, they have no great temptation to steal it. The plagiarists are worse off than the victims. Their inventory depends on the output of others. You have a source of supply all your own.

A practical safety measure, however, is to register it with the Writers Guild. This will cost five dollars for a member and ten dollars for a nonmember. Registration is good for five years, at which time it can be extended.

Just remember that this only registers it. Ideas, plots, or characterizations cannot be copyrighted. The registration is only proof that it was written on that date. Access to the material by the plagiarist must also be proven. If you register a story about a midget horticulturist who has bred a new pink petunia and someone subsequently writes a story about a midget horticulturist who invented a new pink petunia, it is not enough to prove yours was written first. You must also prove that the creator of the other midget horticulturist had access to yours.

They will not buy my material until I have a reputation. So how can I get a reputation unless they buy my material?

Another Catch Twenty-two. If it's any comfort, it's a universal problem. Lack of experience is a handicap in practically every profession except the oldest one. Patently unfair, but not as ridiculous as it sounds on the face of it. Remember the king who always set impossible tasks for his daughter's suitors? This screened out the nerds and dilettantes. All successful comedy writers at one time had no credits or reputation. Eventually, they found someone courageous enough, perceptive enough, or desperate enough to give a neophyte a chance.

Those courageous ones aren't easy to find. They are a rare, fragile breed living in inaccessible places. But if they were easy to find, they'd be gone before you got there.

How did you sell your first script?

I'll tell you, but I doubt that it will help. It took naiveté with unbounded optimism on my part, and a buyer with the same characteristics—a highly unlikely parley. I wrote to every producer of radio shows in Chicago with the information that I had attended Northwestern School of Journalism, had written for the college paper, and would like the opportunity to write for him. Most didn't answer, two were courteous enough to send a printed rejection, and one was desperate enough to let me write on speculation. After three scripts and eight revisions, he finally bought one—and then never used it.

I repeat this improbable story to emphasize the advice I believe every established writer would corroborate. Knock at every door. You never know who is going to be home. There is hardly a writer who hasn't got at least one story of selling to a most improbable source.

How much do I charge?

What the traffic will bear. That, of course, is not always easy to estimate. A new writer is usually satisfied with the minimum, and grateful for anything more.

The M.B.A. (Minimum Basic Agreement) negotiated by the Writers Guild with the producers has minimum fees for most forms of television and screen, including story line, revisions, royalties, etc. The Author's League has minimum fees for stage plays and musicals including option, rehearsal pay, etc.

Just remember that these are *minimums* and you may negotiate for anything more. In that case, or in a case where there are no stipulated fees, it is best to consult with other writers.

A word of caution. Usually you will get your greatest help and cooperation from your fellow writer, but not always in the question of fees. In that area there is always the danger of their ego corrupting the facts. Fees, like the fish that got away and sexual prowess, are most vulnerable to exaggeration. Discussion of all three can give the credulous listener an inferiority complex. But, unlike the second two, fees are usually subject to confirmation.

What are the differences between comedy and drama?

Attitude. Comedy is a subdivision of drama. Its antonym is tragedy. What makes a dramatic story comedic is point of view. I heard a motion picture producer once say that comedy is camera angles.

Terminal diseases may be fuel for comedy, as in "Garbo Talks." A clown performing ludicrous antics can be tragic, as in "The Way of All Flesh." One man's laughter is another man's tears.

I can't give an exact definition of comedy, and have sympathy for anyone who tries. Falling in a mud puddle, losing your clothes in public, a speech impediment, most any kind of embarrassment, is not only a source of amusement to others but, in time, even to the victim. Lenny Bruce once said that comedy is remembered pain.

The early Jerry Lewis burlesque of a spastic's walk offended some. I can't blame them for being offended, nor can I blame those who laughed.

I suppose the standard here is good taste. I can't give a definition of good taste, either, and wouldn't if I could. You usually can't get agreement on a definition in the same household.

What are the chances of getting a successful new comedy series on television?

There are literally thousands of ideas for new series presented to production companies and networks each season, most by established writers, producers, directors, and executives. Of these, hundreds are chosen to move on to the next step of development—a complete script. The networks each choose approximately fifteen to twenty-five of these projects out of which to make a pilot film. Of those, about five will get scheduled on each network. If one or more of these new shows lasts into the next season, it is considered reasonably successful.

These are rough estimates, and cable companies may enlarge the market some, but it serves to demonstrate the odds against initiating a successful series.

Should I write alone or with a partner?

Comedy writers seem to feel a great need for collaboration, even though, outside of autobiography and poetry, it is the most personal of writing.

The generally accepted reason is that the writer of humorous lines needs someone to "bounce" them off of. A stronger reason I believe is because a writer of humor finds himself more vulnerable than other writers. You have avowedly presented yourself as one who can make others laugh. When you're in that spot, it's a blessing to have somebody share the blame as well as the responsibility. (You had best also share the credit, or the collaboration won't last long.)

I have almost always worked alone, for reasons I won't go into here, and in my early career as a comedy writer I was a rarity. When you're standing on the rehearsal stage and a funny line is needed and all eyes turn on you with the, "Well, you're supposed to be the comedy writer" expression, you wish you had at least six partners. You feel like the baseball player up to bat in the ninth with bases loaded, score tied, two outs, and the game being televised nationally. I'm sure he'd share the credit for any possible home run with anyone who would get into the batter's box with him.

Norman Lear, Larry Gelbart, Paul Mazursky, Jules Epstein all work alone but started out with partners. Some comedy teams like Weiskoff and Schiller, I.A.L. Diamond and Billy Wilder, not to mention Gilbert and Sullivan, have lasted longer than most marriages.

Writers of humor in the print media, such as Art Buchwald, S.J. Perelman, and Robert Benchley, worked alone because, I believe, any other way is impractical.

The best reason for a writing partner is moral support. Next to getting married, it's the second most important decision you will ever make.

Maybe the first.

What is your working schedule?

I write three to four hours in the morning. Afternoon I use for meetings, phone calls, letter answering, or any other of the necessary but noncreative chores. I write afternoons only in emergency; evenings and Sundays only because of irresistible inspiration.

Your most productive time may be a different part of the day or night. But I am convinced we can work efficiently and productively not much longer than four hours daily. It is very difficult, except when driven, to keep up concentration for eight hours a day. I think you will find that if the four hours are pure, uncluttered work time, you will outproduce the nine-to-five writer.

Should I go into comedy writing?

No.

I would give the same answer to someone who asked me whether I thought he should climb Mount Everest. And for the same reason. If he feels compelled to ask, he shouldn't leave camp.

·13·

How Much Can You Tell Me About Comedy Writing in No Longer Than I Can Stand on One Foot?

"That is longer than the average attention span, and long enough to explain almost anything less than the Theory of Relativity."

There is a story, perhaps apocryphal, of a caliph who asked the Jewish scholar, Maimonides, to explain the Talmud (many volumes containing the rules of behavior, philosophy, morals, and religious conduct of Judaism) in no longer than he could stand on one foot. (Maimonides's answer, if you didn't already know, was, "Do unto others as you would have them do unto you. The rest is commentary. Go study.")

I decided to ask a few outstanding writers of comedy, all award winners, a similar question on a subject only slightly less incomprehensible.

"How much can you tell me about comedy writing in no longer than I can stand on one foot?" Following are the unedited answers.

ART BUCHWALD *Syndicated Columnist*

You don't write humor, you think humor. Then you write humor. Nobody can teach you. The secret is passed on from one generation to another and I will not tell mine, except to my son.

I.A.L. DIAMOND *Features: The Apartment, Some Like It Hot. One, Two, Three.*

Most humor is based on disparity, especially the disparity between the way man sees himself and the way he actually is. Treat our self-delusions as tragic and you get *Death of a Salesman* and *A Streetcar Named Desire* and *The Iceman Cometh;* treat them as comic, and you have Moliere and Chaplin and Lenny Bruce.

LARRY GELBART *Television: "M*A*S*H." Features: Oh God, Tootsie. Musical: A Funny Thing Happened on the Way to the Forum.*

To write comedy is to view life through a special prescription, reminding us of what we already know, feel, or refuse to admit, and hopefully illuminating those truths, emotions, and denials in an altogether different and entertaining way. And the reward is laughter, the outward expression of a nerve well-struck.

EVERETT GREENBAUM *Television:* "Mr. Peepers," "M*A*S*H," "Andy Griffith Show."*Features: Angel In My Pocket, Good Neighbor Sam.*

Local radio and possibly even TV is full of people who have to go on the air every day, very often with comedy. It is possible to make an arrangement whereby you can write material for them without pay or without credit of authorship.

The point is that you can get a feeling how the material sounds and what works and what doesn't.

When I first went to New York, there was a folk music and comedy show called *Oscar Brand's Brandwagon*. It originated in the city-owned studio atop New York City Hall.

They used my material and to this day I run into actors in Hollywood who remember it and have gone on to successful careers.

The next poverty-ridden radio personality I wrote for was myself, which brings us to another nugget of advice. If you have a hometown (where you can possibly live with your folks) and can't get a foothold in the big city, it might be a good idea to find a station back home. Mine was Buffalo.

Trying New York again, I discovered (Wow! Here's another suggestion coming up) ethnic stations. Big cities have stations catering to all nationalities. I worked my way into a Jewish station, not only writing but also performing for fifteen dollars a week. It more than paid my rent.

I often think when watching Public TV or listening to Public Radio, how lucky a beginner is to have that as a training ground. Most of the people in these facilities work for nothing. They would probably be more than happy to see you.

HAL KANTER *Television:* "Chico and the Man," "Jimmy Stewart Show," "Julia." *Features: Road to Bali, Loving You.*

Writing comedy is a mysterious process that begins long before the craft is established. One sees the world through a prism that distorts truth and, equally, puts sham and pretense into recognizable perspective.

When that sight is recognized and one learns to commit vision to paper, deftly imparting his sight to the reader (or director or players of the piece), the difficulty begins for the comedy writer. That comes with the ongoing struggle to convince others that what you've written is, indeed, funny!

In the commercial theatre, alas, comedy is not necessarily that which makes you laugh; it's what makes the most people laugh.

But there is little in life that provides the author with richer reward than the sound of most people laughing at what he, too, thinks is funny.

NORMAN LEAR *Television:* "All In the Family," "Maude," "Mary Hartman, Mary Hartman." *Features: Divorce American Style, The Night They Raided Minsky's, Cold Turkey.*

The best advice anybody ever gave a writer was to write. And if you believe you see life through the end of the telescope that finds the humor in the most serious of situations, write out of your own experience. I promise you, your mother was funny. So were your uncles and aunts. Use them. And use yourself. Assuming you are human, you are foolish. That is the human condition. Write it.

BOB SCHILLER "I Love Lucy," "All in the Family," "Maude."

The late Ed Gardner (Archie of "Duffy's Tavern"), when asked how he found comedy writers, always answered, "I look for people who think crooked." Now, if you think he was referring to criminal minds, you'll never be a comedy writer. What he was referring to, of course, was the ability to turn a simple thought into a humorous one, or put another way, "thinking funny." Say "hello" to a comedy writer and he/she immediately is trying to come up with any response that isn't the normal one. Thinking off-center. It's a blessing . . . or a curse . . . depending on how successful that person is in capitalizing on this quality. And one is born with it. It can't be taught or acquired. So if you haven't thought of a dozen or more hilarious responses to this paragraph, read no further. Give this book to the class clown and go into the buttonhole business. There are lots of openings. (Okay, okay, so sometimes we miss. Nobody's perfect.)

BOB WEISKOFF "I Love Lucy," "All in the Family," "Maude."

To be a professional comedy writer, be ready for a great deal of rejection, plus lots of advice and "help" from those least qualified to offer it. Everyone knows better than the writer, but only after something has been written. As Fred Allen so aptly asked, "Where is everyone when the paper is blank?"

·14·

Comedy Writing—
The Rites of Passage

*"From the early, bumbling days
of radio to the modern bumbling
days of film."*

It seems strange to realize today that radio comedy was communicated through only one of the senses. To get laughs out of sound alone was not only an imposing challenge, but also served as an effective training course to the many of us who started in that era.

All of our ingenuity was called for to overcome the handicap of sightless comedy. The obvious device of amplifying or diminishing the sound of hoofbeats to denote the approach or departure of a horseman was adapted to indoor drama by having only bare wooden floors. It obviated the contrived entrance of a new character with such awkward dialogue as,

"I think there is someone coming."

"Yes. Here he comes in now."

"Well, if it isn't Uncle Joe."

Instead, the sound man would simulate approaching footsteps with his hands in shoes on a board in front of an open mike and we needed only the line,

"Hello, Uncle Joe."

There wasn't a carpeted floor in all of radio land.

Radio's challenges to humorous inventiveness often led to original and classic bits of comedy. Fibber McGee's closet with its sound of an endless stream of objects falling out every time the door was opened, was one. It is also an excellent example of the rewards of identification in humor. We can bear our own cluttered closets much better when we find his is so much worse.

The creaking sound of the alleged vault in Jack Benny's basement, and the sputtering and coughing sounds of his ancient Maxwell were also standard laugh getters. Another example from this pioneer of radio comedy is the classic joke, that was not only sightless but soundless, about his miserliness. A gunman demanded of him, "Your money or your life." The ensuing silence, while he supposedly thought it over, was one of the most famous laughs in this famous series.

Jack Benny was one of the first in radio to make the transition from stand-up comedian to a character in a situation. The members of his cast, his radio "family," all had definite personalities, and played a reasonably realistic story line. His show, as a matter of fact, was the pioneer and forerunner of much subsequent radio and television comedy.

Another phenomenon from this master of comedy should be noted here. The character he played was miserly and conceited, he underpaid and overworked his employees, and yet he was one of the most lovable characters we had in any medium. The reason was, as explained elsewhere, his well-demonstrated vulnerability. We'll forgive a person almost anything if he's vulnerable, laugh at him if he fails, and love him if he makes a fool of himself trying.

The successful "Fibber McGee and Molly" show was the model for many series of late forties and fifties. Each episode was built around a simple premise (or conflict, to define it more accurately) that was addressed in separate routines by each member of the regular cast, all "funny" people. (These usually included a precocious child, someone with a speech impediment, a man-hungry woman, a woman-hungry man, one very fat and/or thin, one stupid, etc., etc.)

The first year of the "Ozzie and Harriet" radio series in the late forties was patterned after "Fibber McGee." On "Ozzie and Harriet," by making the characters more credible, and adding a third act, the loose collection of routines was transformed into one of the earlier domestic comedies in radio. Later, much later, it was transferred to television where it gradually, by eliminating everything remotely controversial and all impure thoughts or deeds, became almost a parody of itself.

"Duffy's Tavern . . . Where the elite meet to eat, Archie the manager speaking. Duffy ain't here." Duffy, of course, was never there—by design. But, demonstrating the transitory and unstructured state of radio comedy, Archie had never been given a last name and Miss Duffy, originally played by the acclaimed actress Shirley Booth, was never given a first one. By the time the show was well established and these two omissions had become a problem (how did Archie give his name at a court trial, for instance, and what did Duffy call his daughter?), it would have jolted listeners to complete the names.

As in most comedy on radio at that time, there was no full story line as such, merely a premise on which to hang the jokes and routines of the regular members of the cast.

Amazing that the simple story points or springboards (Bob Hope's ineptness with women, Gracie Allen's naiveté, Jack Benny's parsimony) were durable enough for some hundreds of episodes. Let's go backstage to see how this magic was worked.

"Duffy's Tavern" had four to five writers (other shows had up to ten) working full time. Full time meant exactly that; most of our waking hours, with a very occasional stolen evening for a movie or social gathering. The only day off was after the broadcast, which we usually slept away because once a week we worked throught the night.

This was the modus operandi of our and most other comedy shows in radio. The writers would get together, work out a premise based on the guest star (Bing Crosby cajoled to be the Tavern "chanteuse," Lana Turner coaxed for a date, Humphrey Bogart's menace used to get Archie a raise) and the script responsibilities would then be divided. Each writer was responsible for part of a script. (On subsequent shows, "Red Skelton," "Ozzie and Harriet," for instance, every writer wrote a complete script from which the best lines were culled and put together by one person who would usually take credit for the script.)

Two or three days later, we were expected to bring in a "rough." (I remember my naiveté when I found that time was allotted for rewriting before the script had even been written. "Maybe," I said to the head writer, "my script won't need rewriting." He blinked at me as though I had said maybe I would be nominated president by Thursday. Actually, the chances of the second were better than those of the first.)

Then began the tedious work of rewriting, pruning, and

polishing each word of every line into the final script. This ended in an all-night session, the script finished only hours before show time. The pages would be mimeographed and rushed to the studio, where the actors would rehearse for two hours, read it "live" over the network and go home. The cleaning lady then came in, collected the scripts and, with the used plastic coffee cups, dumped them into the waste bin. Three hours after they were finished, the painstakingly worked-over pages were carried out with the trash.

And yet . . .

In some ways it's tougher for the comedy writer today.

We'll get to that later.

On "Duffy's Tavern," after we worked the sixty or seventy hours on the script, we all, except for the head writer, could attend the show only by getting tickets and standing in line to sit in the audience.

There were no writing credits and, except for the season-opening episode which was reviewed in the trade publications. our names were rarely connected with the show. (A commonly used rationale was that if writers were mentioned it would endanger the illusion that the characters were making it up as they went along.) There were exceptions to this. Jack Benny, for instance, as generous in real life as his radio character was purported to be stingy, periodically mentioned his writers. But such incidents of magnanimity were rare.

Our anonymity was sometimes so carefully guarded that after almost two years on "Duffy's Tavern" and three on "Ozzie and Harriet," I was unknown to the members of the cast. On the "Duffy's Tavern" show, we were asked—I suppose to avoid litigation by others or ourselves—to sign a statement affirming that the material was original with us—and was written by the star.

After this description of that sweatshop, salt-mine environment, you are waiting for an explanation of why it might be tougher for the writer of television comedy today.

First, there was an almost insatiable need for material then, with none of the reserves of professional comedy writers to call upon that we have today. Almost anyone who professed to be a comedy writer, or even just someone who made a funny ad lib at an opportune time (I once saw a witty bartender hired by a comedian in the middle of his shift) was given a chance.

Comedy monopolized the airwaves. There were at least twice as many comedy shows as there are today. And with each show having a "stable" of writers, and producing from thirty-six to forty-five episodes a season, there were many job opportunities.

And those few who had the credentials to write comedy usually disdained radio.

So. Anyone who was reasonably competent and would show up for work had a shot.

Another significant advantage for the comedy writer of those days was that he was working closely and directly with one person in authority—usually the star—who could give a speedy and unequivocal yes or no. Today there may be, between submission and acceptance, four different departments, a handful of committees, 5000 miles and as much as three months.

Today one writer, or a team, usually will be responsible for only one to five scripts in a season of twenty-two to twenty-six episodes. (Rather than every writer being involved in every one of a thirty-nine-episode season in those days.) After a story line is accepted, each script, following a rewrite, will then go through another rewrite by the story editor, and perhaps even two or three more before production. At any time during this process, the story line or script might be abandoned entirely.

The highly improved status of the comedy writer today, however, does much to balance the scales. The erstwhile comedy writer was almost never in a position of authority, and usually kept out of all script-editing sessions, Today, the comedy writer is not only allowed into the decision-making process—often as producer—but is welcomed there by those same studio executives who have learned that the best person to edit, to add or omit a line, is the person who can write one.

Although it had the asset of sight as well as sound, television brought with it several disadvantages that again tested our ingenuity.

On radio, we could have forty rampaging elephants, the demolition of a skyscraper, or a bird singing on cue with no added cost or time except what the engineer might need to get the proper sound effects. Not so on TV. An even more serious handicap, in the early days of live television, was giving actors time between scenes for costume changes. (It was a challenging enough problem for all television writers, but we in comedy still had to get our laughs as supporting characters took up a subplot in order to give the leads time to change for the next scene.)

A substantive change in comedy, possibly brought on more by the increased sophistication of the audience than by the change in mediums, was the definite move toward more credible characters and stories. Up to that time, it seemed, radio comedy had been either sketches, domestic comedies where the husband brought the boss home unexpectedly for dinner, or boarding houses with disparate characters where "anything can happen and usually did."

Television comedies had two precedent-shattering innovations. One was that actors were often used, rather than comedians, for the leads; the other was the appearance of romance and sensuality (as opposed to platonic marriages and leering lust).

Writing for one of the earliest television domestic comedies in the late fifties, "My Favorite Husband," with Joan Caulfield and Barry Nelson, and later on, "Mr. Adams and Eve," with Ida Lupino and Howard Duff, we found to our delight and surprise that these legitimate actors could play real love scenes and still get laughs.

Of course, masters of this art, such as Tracy with Hepburn, Gable with Colbert, or Cary Grant with anybody, had been doing it for some time in feature films. But it was gratifying to the television comedy writer, where the symbol of marriage had been a peck on the cheek and twin beds, and sex was always safely adolescent no matter what age, to find that there could be romance in comedy as well as comedy in romance.

In the fifties, the motion picture studios finally decided that television was not going away, that it was a growing source of revenue, and they had best jump on the bandwagon. They soon took over many of the series, both drama and comedy, shooting them on film almost exactly the way motion pictures were shot (except faster and cheaper). Filming not only gave the opportunity for profitable repeats, but also gave motion picture stars, now swarming into the new field, security they didn't have in the unpredictable scariness of live television.

This film technique destroyed, it was said, the "spontaneity" of live television. That seems surprising, since the live comedy had been rehearsed for days, while in film it could be a matter of hours or less after the lines were first said aloud on the sound stage before they were in the can ready for processing. The reason for the loss of spontaneity soon became apparent to those of us who made this transition. There was not only a lot more mechanics and equipment but hordes of new personnel, new bureaucracy, and new rules that descended into the process and took up indomitable positions between the creative people and the product. Studio people, left in the wash of the receding tide of the motion picture industry in the fifties, finally acknowledged the importance of television and stepped in to show the young, adventurous newcomers who had brought it to that point, how it should be done. It had a traumatic effect from which television comedy never fully recovered.

Ironically, the increased physical latitude (no stage waits for costume changes, no breathless run from one set to another) gave us little advantage. We, who had been confined to a studio stage and thirty minutes, and looked forward eagerly to the unrestricted time and space of film, were thwarted by the lugubrious comptroller. There was little solace in the fact that a muffed line or a creaking door could be reshot.

Business people don't like to depend on the vagaries and unpredictability of talent. And comedy is of the most incomprehensible and unpredictable. Accountants prefer the dependable clones of financial success. They feel safe with an inventory of standard products—car chases, monsters, a sexy female cop working undercover, rebellious teenagers, heroes with buttonless shirts, etc.—that they can always depend on to move off the shelf. But that has always been the case. Money is consistently conservative.

Eventually, a process evolved that was a compromise between film and live television, called the three-camera technique. This process, used only in comedy, caught some of the spontaneity by being shot in consecutive scenes and almost continuously in front of an audience. Film from the three cameras, shooting simultaneously, was edited to use the best shots. Time could be taken between scenes for costume and set changes and to reshoot, when necessary, any mishaps. Since this avoided the potential disasters of live performance, and mechanical laughter could be added when the live people neglected to furnish it, it was the best of the only two possible worlds.

While we're on the subject of laughs, this was b.l.t. (that's before laugh track, not bacon, lettuce, and tomato) which presented a challenge that kept the benzedrine in demand. Often hours and hours were spent searching for the line that would ensure the mandatory spontaneous laugh. Yet I've never known a writer of comedy who is not adverse to the laugh track, nor an executive who is not in favor of it.)

During the transitional time after laugh tracks were invented but the shows were still live, the laugh machine, unheard by the audience and cast, was used backstage "to sweeten" the response. Each joke was evaluated as a number one- to four-count laugh. These numbers were penciled in the script and the actors were instructed to wait out that count, to avoid stepping on the sound track laugh. Occasionally, when the live audience saw nothing funny about a joke that a vice-president thought a number four, an eerie silence was created in the studio, while the actor waited out the four-beat count.

Let me interpolate here some notes about a legendary series, "Gilligan's Island," with which I had nothing to do creatively, but with whose fascinating genesis I was indirectly connected in my position then as network supervisor of comedy.

"Gilligan's Island" was, I believe, close to the perfect format for a television comedy series. Seven totally different people from totally different environments, thrown up together on a desert island where anything could happen and by God, usually did. (They could even bring in any character they wanted, by what we came to call, "The Shipwrecked Guest of the Week.")

However, the pilot episode encountered many problems and, in its final form, was received with pronounced apathy by the powers-that-be. One day a programming executive was surprised to find on his desk an audience research report on this project that was supposed to have been abandoned. (I heard two conflicting stories, both from so-called reliable sources, of how this came about. One was that an inefficient underling mistakenly scheduled it for the expensive audience research process. The other story, even more interesting, was that a zealous supporter of the project had, against orders, surreptitiously put the research order through.) In any case, before they had a chance to destroy the report and take disciplinary action against the culprit, someone pointed out that this project, deemed unsuitable for network scheduling, had achieved the most enthusiastic audience response of any project on the schedule. And so was "Gilligan's Island" saved from abortion.

Television became more adult and literate but the dramatic and historic breakthrough that dragged TV comedy—reluctant, fearful, and whimpering— from the land of childlike adults and precocious children into the relatively real world most effectively, was a show called "All in the Family" by a man named Norman Lear and the organization he formed.

It was based on the precedent-shattering assumption that

the lead in a sit-com could have a greater fault than forgetting his wedding anniversary, and comedy could deal with real people—even bigots, and real problems—even abortion.

An even more startling discovery to the network executives was that the television audience could digest and enjoy fare that was more than pap, and enjoyed being treated as adults.

The clever line "Nobody ever went broke underestimating the intelligence of the American public" was, like other lines such as "Let Western Union deliver the messages," "A rock is a rock, a tree is a tree, shoot it in Griffith Park," and "Virtue Always Triumphs," more quotable than accurate.

"All in the Family" and its progeny did much to open new opportunities for the exploration of comedy. Comedy writers, as well as their audiences, have benefited by the larger, more fertile area it has opened for cultivation.

Comedy in the feature motion picture medium should not be substantially different from television—since the physical product, even the equipment, is almost identical—but of course it is. The short, two-reel comedy, so important to the motion picture industry a few years ago, is extinct. The final deathblow was administered by the half-hour television sit-com. (The deftly made drawing room and screwball comedies such as, *The Awful Truth, It Happened One Night,* and *Nothing Sacred,* have also receded into the dim mists of motion picture history. Not by television competition, however. Those delightful comedies spawned a plethora of bad imitations, which not only drove off the audience, but prejudiced them against the entire form.)

A significant difference between television and motion picture comedy is that the latter can deal with subject matter, scenes, and words that are still too sensitive for the home entertainment medium. (Although the area between the two—mainly because of cable and the financial rewards of shock value—is becoming narrower and narrower.) Comedy becomes more sophisticated, more realistic, more effective and, per se, better, as restrictions are lifted.

Historically, writers of humor have always challenged the boundaries of acceptable comment on any subject. In television comedy religion is sacrosanct, politics rarely used as subject matter, but sex is wallowed in, leered at, and vaunted as much as the law and censors will allow. (Censors, traditionally, fit their standards to the most squeamish in the general audience.)

Many of us, in our early days, earned much of our living "switching" risqué jokes. (This was done by replacing the offensive sexual references, while leaving the rest of the joke intact. Sort of like root-canal work.) Thus, we got a double laugh, one from the basic humor of the old standard, and another from those who recalled it in its original form.

By far, however, motion picture comedy differs from television comedy most in the care, time, and money expended on both script and production. This advantage brings with it along with the luxuries of time and available resources, the pressure of the multimillion dollar budget and the tensions of the executive offices. ("They seem to be there," Mervyn LeRoy once bitterly remarked, "to improve it into a flop.")

There are occasionally (only too occasionally, of course) projects that have fought their way through to the rare achievement and minor miracle of good comedy. One of the best and most famous, from the golden era of feature picture comedies, was called *The More the Merrier,* about the housing shortage in wartime Washington. Many years later, this classic was remade into a picture, *Walk, Don't Run,* starring Cary Grant.

The remake was successful but did not measure up to the original. I can say that with impunity because I wrote the adaptation. In adapting this classic, with the luxury of time rather than the treadmill of television from which I had recently come, I learned much, some of which I believe worth passing on.

Although the reviews were generally good, there was one negative note that appeared in many: the comment was that the story was "weak." Surprising since, although the lines and most scenes had been changed, the basic story of the original was used intact.

After some analysis, I found what I believe was the reason for this criticism. The original plot of a young man sharing an apartment with a young woman and older man during the wartime housing shortage in Washington was moved intact to the housing shortage in the Tokyo Olympics. The seemingly small difference, which made the one story "light" while the other was not, was that in the second the protagonist was an athlete competing in the Olympics; in the original he was a soldier about to be shipped overseas.

A reminder, which I shouldn't have needed, of the importance of conflict in comedy; and the more powerful the conflict, the more powerful the comedy is likely to be.

Item number two:

There was one classic piece of business in the original that I felt too delightful to leave out and too perfect to tamper with. When the characters, originally played by Joel McCrea and Jean Arthur, said good night, there was a "petting" scene that I, and I imagine everyone else who saw the picture, would never forget.

Obviously drawn to each other, they kept up a stream of mindless chatter while pretending to ignore the very apparent physical attraction.

It was a romantic, sensual, and yet very funny scene, both seemingly engrossed in the conversation and acting totally unaware of what their hands and lips were doing.

In the second version, the director had added a seemingly innocuous "Don't!" to her dialogue as she pushed off his hands. With that single word, he made an ordinary scene out of an inspired bit of romantic comedy. Moral: Only those aware of how fragile comedy is, and competent to understand its workings, should tinker with the machinery.

The apparent ease and grace with which Cary Grant wears

clothes comes from the same care, good judgment, and perception with which he reads lines. I had the opportunity to learn about both.

I had to prepare for my trip to Japan by replenishing my usually inadequate wardrobe. I solved it by finding a hopsack cloth suit which, I was assured, would not show the abuse I usually gave to clothes, and ordered three identical suits, two in shades of gray and one in blue. It seemed a shrewd solution to a pesky problem. I did not know at the time that I would be spending every day for two months, and every evening at dinner with one of the best-dressed men in America. I thought Cary Grant didn't notice; I realized later it was not his lack of observation, but his thoughtfulness and diplomacy.

Late one afternoon while revising the script, this master of light comedy, who weighed the tiniest motivation with the care and precision of a classical actor at the Old Vic, questioned the predicament of the character he was playing.

"Why," he asked, "didn't this man make a hotel reservation?"

"He forgot," I said, giving what I thought was an adequate explanation.

"I don't play that kind of character," he said, with the impatience that came from the long, tense hours we were working. "I don't play the kind of man who wears hopsack suits and doesn't make hotel reservations."

I believe that I learned a lot about comedy from Cary Grant, but I have to admit that my wardrobe has not improved.

If there is something to be learned from this partial retrospective on the many changing faces of comedy, it is to learn your craft. When I first started in the comedy field and the stand-up comic was dominant, the facile writer of the two-line joke was in the most enviable position, until the mainstream of comedy changed to character and situation and he fell by the wayside—unless he had learned his craft.

I have mentioned fine writers who got their start writing

the two-line jokes of that era, but successfully made the transition. They were able not only to keep up with the changing trends, but to take advantage of all the improvements of the electronic media—because the basics of humor are the same in any form, and they had mastered those fundamentals. Those who didn't have faded away into obsolescence.

So . . . learn your craft.

And how do you learn it? Mostly by doing. You will learn some by watching how others do it, some by profiting from the experience of others, which is one of the purposes of this book. But mostly by doing it yourself, by trial and error, and learning the fundamentals until they become second nature to you. It may not get any easier—the more you learn, the more adept you become, the higher your standards get—but I promise you your work will get better.

You will stumble, fumble, rewrite, and curse, until—without warning—one day you will look at a page with your own words and want to shout in exhilaration, "Hey, that's good!" Not every line, not every time. Nobody does it every time, every line. But if you work at it, if you have that perception of the incongruous and the tendency to make a playful judgment, that moment will come more and more often.

One final word, in case you missed it.

Learn your craft.

·15·

The Comedy Writer's Survival Kit

"To be opened only in case of emergency, which will probably be not less than three times a day."

Do you feel inadequate, frustrated, self-doubting, untalented (whatever made you think you had talent?), self-pitying (how come it's so hard for you and so easy for everybody else?), and hopeless (maybe it's not too late to change your mind about selling appliances for your father-in-law). Relax. It happens to everybody. It goes with the territory. Ask the best and most successful. Those interviews you read about the happily fulfilled writer who can't wait to get to the typewriter are given either in the moment of euphoria after a hit, or are lies he's telling to cover up his own feelings of inadequacy, frustration, and self-doubt.

Remember, things are tough all over.

Don't believe everything you hear—not even from writers. When I was younger and just beginning to be aware of the opposite sex, I felt, as I guess most of us did, inadequate, inferior, and unattractive. I was further frustrated when I heard the frequent stories from my peers about the girls—numerous, and always beautiful—who readily and enthusiastically succumbed to their ready wit and manly charms. I listened, sinking even deeper in the quagmire of inadequacy, while they told me how many, how often, and how long.

If I had only known then that they were lying. (And if one or two weren't, it was even more important not to listen.)

Some writers likewise love to regale other writers about the assignments they turned down, the fees they got, and how many producers they told what to do with suggestions.

Usually other writers are of the greatest help. They offer a sympathetic ear, market information, and unfailing commiseration to your diatribes about agents. But, at the risk of being disloyal to my own kind. . . .

Don't confine your social life exclusively to comedy writers. If they are your only area of communication in the real world, it becomes incestuous—with many of the dire consequences of incest.

You will find that in a social environment of only writers, you are usually envied when you are successful and patronized when you're not. Both reactions are equally undesirable. So make the mix of your social life both more variable and safer by including plumbers, pastry cooks, hustlers, lawyers, even actors and producers. Except dentists—they all want to be comedy writers.

Beware of people in three-piece suits who have attaché cases full of demographics. The suit is pure wool, the attaché case genuine leather, but the information which purports to tell you what people are listening to and laughing at was collected from other people with nothing more interesting to do with their time than fill out survey questionnaires. And whose reactions are analyzed by other people sitting on the beach at Malibu until Junior comes back with the sailboat.

Audience reaction demographics were concocted by executives in their incessant battle to take all chance out of the entertainment field. Which means avoiding originality and ignoring talent to make it businesslike (in show business a sacrosanct virtue) and keep it away from the corruptive influence of those unmanageable artists who don't have proper respect for the Dow Jones averages. (Another of my complaints is calling our profession "the industry" or "show business." "Show business," I remember Ed Wynn saying, "is seeing that there are paper towels in the rest rooms. What's done on that stage is art.")

Quote demographics when they are favorable; when they are unfavorable, quote the above.

Keep in good physical condition.

That is, of course, important to anyone in any occupation. In the trade of weaving words into funny lines and amusing situations, conditioning is almost as essential as to a professional athlete.

You need energy to write, surprisingly more than you would think. Most craftsmen, laborers, and professionals can still get through the day even when tired, hung over, or just under the weather. You, the comedy writer, need to be at all times brighter and sharper than your audience to stay ahead of them. Or you'll both be bored out of your gourds.

So jog, play tennis, use the exercycle, anything that will keep you in condition. Like the pitcher in the big game, you need to be rested, in top shape, and prepared. Because there's always some son-of-a-bitch warming up in the bull pen.

While you're getting your start, it's best to have a day job. After you have your start, avoid any other financial pursuits. They will take up too much of your time, may be more profitable, and almost certainly more fun.

It is not essential—but almost—that you have an understanding spouse or lover.

Another desirable but nonessential idea is to keep your helpmate in awe. This can be accomplished by always acting introspective and profound. (The superficial device of smoking a pipe has fallen into disrepute. Pipes keep going out and are conducive to lip cancer. Besides, we're still conditioned to feel a pipe doesn't become women writers.)

It also helps to throw a tantrum once in awhile—a small one, just big enough to get attention, but not so large as to send her home to her mother. (Please believe that I'm not sexist; it's just that I think "his or hers" makes for awkward sentence structure.)

But the best thing, of course, is to make a lot of money. Otherwise, they not only don't understand why you have to straighten out the drawers and check the temperature in your hometown, but expect you to carry out the garbage as long as you aren't doing anything anyhow.

Be kind to yourself.

You are a vulnerable artist in an uncaring competitive world. It's the sympathetic sort of part usually played by someone like Robert Redford. Redford was unavailable, so please be kind to his understudy.

When you can't think of anything funny to say, don't say it. When you can't think of anything funny to write, write it anyhow. That's your job. It's how you pay your bills.

Then take the unsuccessful version and turn it upside down. Find another controversy and take another point of view and turn that upside down. If it still doesn't work, the next day find another controversy, take another point of view. . . .

When you write comedy for a living, just as when you sell shoes or run a bank, you can't take time off just because you're not in the mood. You try to think of funny things when you're told your house has termites, or you're on your way to the dentist, or your eccentric aunt left a suicide note and went to the movies—or all three. Unless you're independently wealthy, you put it out of your mind and just go and write. . . .

That may, finally, be the *real* mark of the professional.

Don't promise and don't apologize.

No promises, no expectations. The prefatory, "Here's a funny story," is usually met with a challenging, "Let's see" attitude. Anyone who has been introduced with, "This is a very witty person," is familiar with the "We dare you" look.

Like the boast of being a great lover, it leaves you vulnerable to a witnessed humiliation. Don't promise them anything and if they're not grateful, at least they won't be disappointed. It is a contest to make them laugh, but don't let them know that. They can smell the sweat of fear way back to the twenty-second row.

Even if you have failed, don't apologize. They may not know you've failed. And if they do, they may think it's their fault. Which may not be true, but at least it's better than thinking it's yours. That's probably the basic reason for the laugh track in television comedy. It says how dare you not laugh when all these other bright people think it's so hilarious?

The writer of comedy lines (and the speaker of those lines) must always stay in command of the situation. People lose confidence in a commander who makes excuses. Making excuses is a bid for sympathy, and sympathy may bring a handout, tears, maybe even love, but it never gets laughs.

Never explain your joke. If it can't stand on its own two feet, give it up as a casualty. Some comedians insist on a decent burial ("What are you, an audience or a jury?" "That's the last time I buy a joke from my brother-in-law.") But whatever you do, don't try to explain why the joke is funny. It's a lost cause. You're giving up spontaneity and surprise to start with; you are asking for understanding and they are reluctant to give that even to relatives and loved ones. And you're just a hired hand.

Keep in mind that what you write is never as good as you thought it would be, rarely as bad as you think it is.

Don't tell people you are a comedy writer. It's the only profession outside of private detective for which proof is demanded on the spot.

Never team up with a writer going through a divorce.
Never team up with a writer about to get married.
Never team up with a writer with whom you are contemplating either.
Never team up with a writer who is oversexed or undernourished.

Don't try to ad-lib with a comic. He can remember much faster than you can think.

Don't take comedy too seriously. Each is an antidote for the other. In proportions any larger than the safe capacity for human consumption, they cancel each other out.

There is no such thing as a bad joke or a bad scene. There are only jokes and scenes that don't work. It's not your fault. Just fix it or discard it. There are thousands of ways to compose any line, but only a few of them work. Once you've had the courage to take on those odds, you can congratulate yourself when you've succeeded and still be proud when you fail.

When you witness excellent comedy writing, don't be intimidated; and don't be arrogant about bad. You will at times do both. If you do only one, it will surely be the latter.

There is no doubt that the best writer in the world sometimes writes bad lines. There's no doubt that you have written some good lines. It is arguable, therefore, that at times you write better than the best writer in the world.

Be good to yourself. You're the only writer in the room.

·16·

Birth of a Television Comedy Series

*"It's not an immaculate conception, no matter
what they say. There are labor pains,
a high mortality rate, sleepless nights and
plenty of dirty diapers to change. But if
you're very, very lucky, it might support you
in your old age."*

I chose the pilot script of the television series "Bewitched" to use as a specimen in analyzing television comedy for obvious reasons. First, I wrote it. The screen credit also includes "created by," a delineation that always embarrassed me, since I was brought up to believe that this is a function possessed solely by a superior being. But the word doesn't awe or intimidate those lesser beings who decide on screen credits. They believe, for instance, that the phenomenon of bringing, say, "Love Boat" to the television screen was only slightly less portentous than the incident of the Garden of Eden. Further evidence of the awe in which they hold any new series is that the list of guidelines is reverently called "the bible." They also go to a church called Audience Research Analysis, the priests are network executives, the prophets are the agents, and that's as far as I care to go with the analogy.

But, by whatever name, my close involvement will enable me to describe each step, frustration, change, and reason or lack of reason for it, from the first conference to the final shooting script of the pilot episode. Since it was produced for nine years and is still being replayed in almost every country in the world, and in most of the major languages, I assume that the reader will be familiar with it.

In the beginning, before there was a "Bewitched," there was a Hollywood restaurant called Musso Franks, noted then if not now, as one of the premier deal-making places to do lunch. Harry Ackerman, an executive of the television arm of Columbia Pictures, and I were discussing ideas and concepts for a possible new television series. Several were brought up, but the one we both reacted to enthusiastically was that of a witch who comes to earth and lives as a mortal.

(Note: There has since been much published and public controversy about who of several were initially responsible for the idea, a contretemps that I carefully stayed out of. I felt the entire question was academic. First, because I was already receiving contractual and screen credit, and second, because the idea of a witch living as a mortal was born long before that lunch at Musso Franks. It has been used in Greek mythology, in fairy tales, in novels, on the stage, and in motion pictures. The only real originality, I'm quite willing to confess, was that "Bewitched" was the first to adapt the concept successfully to the television screen.)

The next step was to fashion the leading characters and the setting. There wasn't much choice in this area. In the TV of the sixties, the leading woman had to be a widow, a wife, or a virgin. A divorced woman was taboo, unless she was a supporting character and very funny to boot.

So our star had to have a husband. Again, very little choice. By tradition, he had to be a WASP who loved his mother and was slightly retarded in a charming way. His occupation— he had to be white collar, with enough money so that poverty was never hinted at, but not so much money as to lose story premises. We picked advertising executive, second in popularity only to real estate salesman. These occupations were desirable because they gave our co-star character free time to come home in the middle of the day when needed, and the ability to be someplace where he could be reached by phone when his wife had a funny domestic problem.

(Exceptions, such as Jackie Gleason being a bus driver, or Lucy's husband being a Cuban bandleader, were only allowed because the star had clout enough to demand them. Ozzie, on the other hand, of "Ozzie and Harriet" never had a job or an office, or anywhere to go for that matter, except next door where there were funny neighbors amply supplied with one-liners.)

These decisions are not as superficial as they sound. The setting in a television series—both comedy and dramatic— must be a fertile ground for the twenty-six or so story premises needed each season. That is why police stations, newspaper offices and hospitals are among the most frequently used.

The leading character's home in a comedy, however, was the almost obligatory little house in the suburbs. (Which rarely has an entry hall, so that people coming in and going out never disappear from view. Usually they don't knock. Answering a door takes up too much production and screen time.)

The next step was a story line. This, in a pilot script, is crucial. It must establish all the main characters, the environment, the basic conflict, and still have a story. As we go through the script, I'll explain how these and other problems were dealt with.

At this point it might be informative to recount some of the seemingly trivial and superficial problems and incidents that occurred on the long road from concept to airing of this series—things that may seem irrelevant, but strongly influenced the final product.

The excellent cast of "Bewitched" contributed greatly to its success. I would like to take at least partial credit for the brilliant casting, but I can't. My first choice for the part of Samantha was Tammy Grimes.

Just after finishing the first draft of the pilot script, I saw Tammy Grimes in an unmemorable movie. Immediately, I felt that the elf-like and ethereal quality of this fine actress was perfect for a witch who lived as a mortal. Bill Dozier, head of Screen Gems at the time, agreed enthusiastically. Not only that, but Tammy was a friend of his, and he happened to know she was vacationing on the west coast at the time. So that very morning, Bill and I traveled out to Malibu, script in hand, to try to interest Tammy Grimes in our project.

It would make a better story to relate that she didn't like the concept. She did. She would happily do the pilot. Except that she was planning to do a musical version of Noel Coward's *Blithe Spirit* and wouldn't be available until the next season. I believed strongly enough in my choice to have been willing to wait, but the studio already had the pilot on their agenda for the coming season.

A few days later, the daughter of the talented actor Robert Montgomery, who was already making a name for herself as an actress, came to the office of Screen Gems with her husband,

Bill Asher, with an idea they had for a television series. Harry Ackerman, without explanation, handed them the rough draft of "Bewitched." They took the script home, called back a few hours later and said they would like to do it.

So, in that series of coincidences and happenstances we cast, I believe, the best possible choice for our lead.

Another contribution for which I would like to take credit but can't. For some time I had been seeking for an interesting, unique gesture with which Samantha would manifest her magic. (A creator's work is never done.) At one of the meetings, Bill Asher, who would direct the first year of the series and produce the rest, came in with the news that one of the minor accomplishments of his talented wife was that she could twitch her nose. So was born the legend.

Then, an occurrence that merely proves the old show business law that anything that can happen, will. While on a family visit to Chicago, I was called with two pieces of news. The ABC network had accepted the series for the new season, and our star was pregnant.

When I returned to California, we had meetings to solve the problem—not the first or last time grandiloquent ventures in show business were upset by biological functions of the star. The solution held most in favor was to have the character, Samantha, go through the pregnancy and birth along with the actress, Elizabeth, playing her. I resisted this. (Although I was reminded that, in my prospectus, I had suggested that in coming seasons the series might be enlivened by the birth of a half-witch, half-mortal child.) I remember, after a break in the meeting, blurting out an incredulous, "A pregnant witch?!"

It was finally decided that we "shoot around" the pregnancy. That is, the production was to move as fast as possible and then, when Liz started to show evidence of her oncoming motherhood, to shoot only close-ups, over-the shoulder shots, and long shots where a double could be used. In this way, they were able to get quite a few episodes completed, until Liz went almost directly from the sound stage to the hospital. In an unbelievably short time she was back on the stage, and if she hadn't had an infant to prove it, it would have been difficult to believe the reason for her hiatus. So, to use two clichés in the same sentence, the star was a trouper and the show went on. (The next time our star was pregnant, her screen character imitated life and both progressed through the pregnancies, and the births together.)

Finally, I encountered a very serious problem. After I finished the first draft I realized that, because the protagonist can solve any problems with a twitch of her nose, it was going to be difficult if not impossible to sustain suspense. In short, I had no conflict.

Conflict, the indispensable element, is one of the first lessons in storytelling. It is mentioned, emphasized, repeated in any book on writing. Yet the most experienced of us sometimes need reminding. In this long-running television series, it was put in almost as an afterthought.

I wrestled with the problem. Although I knew my pilot script was interesting and entertaining, I knew that the concept lacked the staying power needed for a long series without a basic conflict. It was finally solved, as you will see in the following script, by the witch's husband objecting strongly to witchcraft, and extracting a promise from her that she will kick the habit. I made a note that in future scripts magic should solve problems only as a last resort, for the same reason. It seems like a slight point, yet it might have been the difference between a one-season series and a long-running hit.

The above anecdotes are intended to demonstrate what can happen to a new television series on the way to air. If nothing more, they prepare you for the unexpected and unpredictable, which, in television production, are the only things that can be expected or predicted. The problems of writing the actual pilot script are only slightly more predictable. The prospectus and script are shown in the following pages as they were used in the production. The italics are for you. They show the problems, how they were solved if they were solved, and the reasons, when there were reasons.

A prospectus is almost always done for potential sponsors of a new series. It is primarily a selling function, a hustle, although enough is described about the contents, style, and aims to give the sponsor a general idea of what the series is about.

This differs from what is called "the bible," which is written after the show has been sold and scheduled, and is mainly for the use of writers of future episodes. The bible describes the main characters, explains their functions, and lays out the ground rules. Thus it will carefully point out the taboos, plus the undesirable as well as desirable character traits and plot lines. The bible is for prospective writers; the prospectus is for prospective clients. Here is the latter for "Bewitched."

Prospectus for a Television Series
"Bewitched"

He is the clean-cut, well-groomed, promising young advertising executive you see in bunches on the New Haven 5:37 going up to Connecticut. Once he has divested himself of the charcoal grey suit and the black attaché case, however, he becomes an individualistic, charming, sometimes-impatient, usually affectionate, often-critical, intermittently appreciative, irritating, likable—in short, very normal—husband.

(The operative word here is "normal." That is, what in those days was considered normal in television, which excluded anyone poor, handicapped, or unattractive.)

She is the attractive young wife whom you see meeting him in the station wagon—that is, when she isn't angry at him—which is no more or less often than any self-respecting young wife is angry at her intermittently critical, usually affectionate young husband.

They have, added to the usual adjustments every young couple must make, one unusual one—she is a witch. No, that is not a typographical error, it's spelled with a *w*.

Well! You can imagine the problems that causes. Or perhaps you can't. But that doesn't matter, because we have imaginative writers who can.

(That last paragraph is pretty cutesy. I wouldn't write it now and it's a temptation to cut it, but I think accuracy is more important than vanity.)

So, added to the problems any young bride has, we have a girl who was learning how to brew rare herbs and strange incantations, while others were studying home economics. While the others were doing the Bossa Nova and copying recipes for an upside-down cake, she was practicing levitation and making people disappear.

Doesn't seem much of a problem, does it? How often has your wife said, "I'm only human, you know," or "I've only got two hands." Well, our girl is not bound by either of these restrictions, On the other hand, her education and background have hardly prepared her for the very demanding, highly specialized, almost impossibly difficult role of Connecticut housewife.

(Identification—a strong selling point in television. And, in the use of comedy, rightfully so. Okay, okay, so it's not exactly feminist. This was some time ago when I was still an overtrained chauvinist male.)

Even the considerable advantage of having supernatural powers (you have no idea how handy that can be in avoiding dishpan hands and pesky door-to-door salesmen) is of little help to her because she has solemnly promised—well, as solemnly as she can—that she will not make use of these powers. Obviously the practice of witchcraft is not seemly in the wife of a young executive with ambitions to gain a position professionally on Madison Avenue and socially in Westport.

(Conflict—selling point number two.)

Also, if she is able to abstain from witchcraft for a certain prescribed period of time, she will become mortal—a very desirable state for a young witch who is hopelessly in love with a mortal and wants very much to live a normal life as his normal wife. However, the temptation for using witchcraft is well-nigh irresistible (for our purposes it *is* irresistible) in trying to cope with the mechanics of living as an average young housewife. Look how difficult it is just to give up smoking.

The conflict in general, therefore, is the usual one of a young couple's adjustment to each other, her problem of adjusting to a normal life, embellished by her endeavors to become normal.

What will the stories be like? Well, they will have all the more desirable elements of a domestic comedy, plus the above intriguing complications.

(And prove to the sponsor that the series has potential for longevity.)

To indicate a few:
A. A young witch trying to fit into the conventional status of the suburban housewife.
B. The in-laws coming to dinner.
C. Her mother coming to dinner (she's a witch, remember, but it's still her own mother).
D. The superstitious client's wife who believes in astrology, witchcraft, and fortune telling, forcing Liz to take the opposite side.

E. A costume ball with some of her supernatural friends and relatives insisting on attending (you can't tell the witches from the mortals without a score card).

F. An absent-minded lapse into witchcraft at a very inopportune time.

G. Her mother insists on meeting her mother-in-law and promises to behave nomally—you are afraid she won't—and she doesn't.

H. The professional magician performing at the Charity Ball who drafts Liz as his subject, and she inadvertently out-mystifies him.

I. Her husband trying to explain to his mother how the ineradicable spot got out of the rug; and a well-meaning friend wants to bottle the great spot remover and market it.

J. Hallowe'en, of course (when that witch comes to the door, trick or treating, you're never sure she's wearing a costume).

K. The neighbor child who accidentally happens upon a genuine incantation and every time the child repeats it, an increasingly angry witch keeps reappearing.

. . . et cetera, et cetera, and always underlying every problem the temptation to lapse into witchcraft, and her husband's admonitions against it.

Fertile areas for stories are the background of commuter suburbanite living, if you are familiar with it; the advertising business if you aren't self-conscious about it, and a bewitched—and bewitching—housewife in this setting if you can imagine it.

(Some of these were used as stories, some as springboards for stories, some not at all. The obvious purpose is to show the prospective client the type of stories, as well as the plentiful supply.)

The supporting cast of characters also offers a wealth of material:

Her mother—a sophisticated, modern witch.

Her father—a sweet, absent-minded, confused witch (there he was on the Fourth of July with pumpkins under his arm), who is afraid to go out in daylight because he might meet people.

(This character was played by Maurice Evans, and not at all portrayed confused or bumbling as described above. A good example of how a character can be adapted to a desirable actor or vice versa to allow more productive story lines. The above description better fits another character played by Paul Lynde.)

His mother, who can trace her lineage back to the May-flower—and often does—in sharp contrast to that of his matter-of-fact, down-to-earth (if you'll pardon the expression) mother-in-law.

His younger sister, a sweet, outspoken teenager who "digs" Liz.

(She never appeared in the series. Par for the course. A well-written series is elastic and continually changing. Projected characters, if they don't work out, are minimized, dropped, or sometimes aborted, as was this one. On the other hand, characters never planned, who are used once and fit in well with the story and entertainment values, are used more and more often, more and more fully, and sometimes become what we call "running" characters. Examples of the latter are Samantha's next door neighbor and husband. (The "Fonz" is an example of a supporting character taking over a show.)

His older sister, basically nice (we have no villains in this series), who is valiantly trying to help Liz fit into Connecticut society.

(Never appeared in the series. See above.)

His bachelor friend—they went through school, the army

and now the advertising business together. He knows all the answers but is unfamiliar with some of the questions.

(As you will see, he had an important scene in the pilot script. Then, although we'd expected the character to be important, he was virtually dropped from the series. Most of the story needs he was expected to fill were taken over by the character, "Larry," portrayed by David White, Darrin's employer.)

We fill in the background with a motley assortment of her relatives and friends of the other world, their neighbors, his office (including his superior who likes to meet the young executives' wives to see if they are proper helpmates) and assorted clients.

(A grab bag to take in any characters writers might dream up in future scripts.)

These, in general, and only hitting the high spots, are the situations, people, problems, and background of our series. Enough, certainly, to offer interesting stories for at least five years, which is the minimum length of time we expect this series to run.

("Five years" was said with the exaggerated bombast of a used car salesman. By God, it lasted nine. Which shows you even used cars and, more rarely, television series sometimes live up to their promises.)

BEWITCHED

*Anatomy of a
Television Pilot Script*

Here now is the original script for the pilot of the television series "Bewitched." Like the prospectus, it has been interspersed with comments, in italics, to point out the problems we encountered, the solutions to those problems (if they were solved), the choices we made, and the reasons and explanations—when they are relevant—for certain scenes, characterizations, and story points.

One last note. Although this was called the "revised final" draft, no script is really final until, curiously, *after* it is shot. In this script you will notice the heroine was named Cassandra. Somewhere between this script and the sound stage, it was changed to Samantha. At this time I no longer remember why. I doubt that it was for any significant reason.

BEWITCHED

A half-hour Pilot Script.

Written by Sol Saks

FADE IN:

INT. DEPARTMENT STORE—DAY

1   ANGLE   1

> NARRATOR
>
> Once upon a time . . .

We discover CASSANDRA, attractively dressed in tailored suit, shopping.

> NARRATOR
>
> . . . there was a typical American girl . . . who happened to bump into . . .

We see her literally bump into DARRIN. They are obviously taken with each other although no words are spoken. She turns for a last glance as she walks away. He appreciatively sizes her up from the top of her well-groomed head to her tiny toes.

> NARRATOR
>
> . . . a typical red-blooded American boy.

DISSOLVE TO:

INT. SAME STORE

2   CASS   2

is looking closely, examining a mannequin, and as she moves around she comes almost nose to nose with DARRIN examining it from the other side.

> NARRATOR
>
> And she bumped into him . . .

DISSOLVE TO:

INT. SAME STORE

3   CASS   3

Coming around counter, arms full of packages, she bumps into DARRIN again and drops packages. He helps her pick them up.

NARRATOR
And bumped into him . . .

DISSOLVE TO:

INT. SAME STORE
4   CASS   4
coming into revolving door. Darrin, coming from other direction, without seeing, gets into same section of door with her.
They start all around together and start making another round
trip as others wait for opening.

NARRATOR
And bumped into him . . .

DISSOLVE TO:

INT. RESTAURANT—DAY
5   DARRIN AND CASS   5
at the table together, animatedly talking.

NARRATOR
So they decided they'd better sit down and talk this
over before they had an accident.

DISSOLVE TO:

INT. DANCE FLOOR—NIGHT
6   DARRIN AND CASS   6

NARRATOR
They became good friends.

DISSOLVE TO:

EXT. OPEN CONVERTIBLE—NIGHT
7   DARRIN AND CASS   7
kissing in open convertible.

NARRATOR
They found they had a lot of interests in common.

DISSOLVE TO:

INT. MOVIE
8   DARRIN AND CASS   8
    kissing.

NARRATOR
Movies.

DISSOLVE TO:

INT. LIVING ROOM
9   MED. SHOT   9
    TV set is on. Darrin and Cass kissing on couch.

NARRATOR
Television.

DISSOLVE TO:

EXT. GRASS—DAY
10   DARRIN AND CASS   10
    on grass, kissing. A transistor radio is announcing a used-car
    sale.

NARRATOR
Radio.

DISSOLVE TO:

EXT. BRIDGE—NIGHT
11   DARRIN AND CASS   11
    necking in convertible under bridge.

NARRATOR
Bridges.

DISSOLVE TO:

EXT. HIGHWAY—DAY

12   DARRIN AND CASS   12
      on highway in car, waiting as train passes.

                    NARRATOR
      Trains.
They are kissing. They hold kiss until train passes and horns start honking.

                    NARRATOR
      And when the boy found the girl attractive, desirable, irresistible, he did what any red-blooded American boy would do. He asked her to marry him.

DISSOLVE TO:

INT. JUSTICE OF THE PEACE OFFICE

13   J.P.   13
      performing wedding ceremony.

                    NARRATOR
      They had a typical wedding . . .

DISSOLVE TO:

EXT. HIGHWAY—DAY

14   CAR   14
      with "Just Married" sign going down highway.

                    NARRATOR
      Went on a typical honeymoon.

DISSOLVE TO:

INT. BRIDAL SUITE—NIGHT

15   DARRIN   15
      —in dressing gown—is sipping champagne and impatiently watching door.

CUT TO:

INT. BEDROOM
16 CASS   16
—in lovely nightgown—fixing her hair.

NARRATOR
In a typical bridal suite . . . *Except.*
Cass looks around the room, sees her negligee on the bed. She
makes a slight motion.

MUSIC: STING. The negligee flies across the room to her
waiting hand.

NARRATOR
It so happens that *this* girl is a witch.
Cass is holding back a lock of hair with one hand as she reaches
for a hairbrush. The brush is too far away to reach. Cass makes
another motion.

MUSIC: STING. The brush moves within convenient distance.
She takes it and starts to calmly brush her hair.

BILLBOARD

MAIN TITLE

CREDITS

FADE OUT

*(This part is what is sometimes called the "teaser," but in this in-
stance is closer to another standard equipment scene known among
writers as the "meet-cute." It was almost obligatory in any romantic
comedy during the golden days of romantic comedies on the screen.
When Doris Day and Rock Hudson starred in a movie, you knew they
had to fall in love. A first ranking star never falls in love with less
than a co-star except in tragedies. So the writer of those comedies
used all his ingenuity to make the predictable sound fresh. The most
famous meet-cute, judged best by many writers of the genre, was that
of Claudette Colbert and Gary Cooper in "Bluebeard's Eighth*

Wife." She slept in only the top of pajamas, resented paying for the unused bottoms and, while shopping for some, ran into Gary Cooper who used only the bottoms.

The above "Bewitched" meet-cute is not the best, but it more than adequately served the purpose. They had to meet, fall in love, get married, and disclose that she was a witch. According to my notes, it was done in one minute forty-five seconds screen time, which merely shows competence, not talent. This is still an art form, not the Olympics.

FADE IN:

INT. BRIDAL SUITE—NIGHT

17   CASS   17

is just making final pats to her hair.

MUSIC: STING. Curtains flutter and fly. There is a clap of thunder and a more mature witch (MOTHER) materializes before our eyes.

Another obligatory scene. We had to introduce and establish Mother, a character we hoped would be an important running character as well as a springboard for plot lines. At this time, we didn't know we were going to get the consummate actress, Agnes Moorhead, to help achieve our goal.

CASS

Mother!

MOTHER

Sorry about the racket, but I was in a—sixty-five dollars a day for *this?*

CASS

Mother, what are you doing here?

MOTHER

What am *I* doing here?! What are *you* doing here?

CASS

I'm married.

MOTHER

I know! . . . Let you out of my sight for one minute
. . . Well, hold on to me and we'll be home before
. . .

CASS

I don't want to go, Mother.

MOTHER

I was afraid of that. He's got a spell over you, huh?
Those male witches are the worst kind. Now let's see
. . .

CASS

Mother, he's not a witch.

MOTHER

What?!

CASS

He happens to be, if you'll excuse the expression, a
normal, mortal, human being.

MOTHER

Ah, that's easy, then. I'll just have him trip over a rug
and break an arm.

CASS

Mother.

MOTHER

Or maybe I'll give him a little stomachache. I love
when doctors start poking, trying to figure out what it
is.

CASS

Mother.

MOTHER

Or maybe I'll turn him into a—

CASS
(interrupts)
Mother, you'll leave him alone—he's a dear, sweet, wonderful, perfectly marvelous man.

MOTHER
My poor baby. He sounds horrible. Now don't worry, dear
. . . I'll get you out of here and—

CASS
I'm not going.

MOTHER
Oh, really—How would you like to spend your wedding
night with a bull frog?

CASS
Mother, you wouldn't—Don't you understand—I'm happy with him.

MOTHER
Don't talk to your mother like that. I'll tell you when
you're happy.

CASS
(Looking off into space)
He's coming in.

CUT TO:

INT. SITTING ROOM
18   DARRIN   18
sets down champagne glass and starts toward bedroom door.

CUT TO:

INT. BEDROOM
19   CASS AND MOTHER   19

MOTHER
I'll take care of that.
(lifts hand)

> CASS
>
> Easy, now!

> MOTHER
>
> I'm not going to hurt him.

CUT TO:

INT. LOBBY

20   DARRIN   20

—walking toward bedroom door—suddenly finds himself in lobby, still walking, and still dressed in pajamas and dressing gown. DESK CLERK looks up, startled. Darrin looks around bewilderedly. Shakes his head.

> DARRIN
> (sheepishly)
>
> Must be the champagne.

He starts toward stairs.

> CLERK
>
> Wow—some honeymoon!

CUT TO:

This mother and daughter scene is mostly exposition. To keep exposition from being dull is an even greater problem in comedy than in other forms of drama. It can be made more palatable by interspersing it with conflict or comedy. Here we used both.

"Never give exposition," I remember a veteran writer saying, "except in anger" . . . or schtick.

INT. BEDROOM

21   ANGLE ON CASS   21

(fuming) CAMERA PULLS BACK to reveal Mother.

> MOTHER
>
> . . . A girl with your advantages and bringing up . . . You were eighteen before you were allowed to stay out after sunrise . . . Bringing scandal to a fine family name by marrying a normal human being.

CUT TO:

Not an explosive laugh by any means but contains two essentials of humor; comedy with a statement. The comedy is the unexpected reversal of prejudice. The statement is antibigotry.

INT. SITTING ROOM

22 DARRIN   22
has just come back in. He's still a little bewildered. He looks with distrust at the champagne. Smells the bottle.

CUT TO:

INT. BEDROOM

23 CASS AND MOTHER   23

> CASS
> Mother, if you could only understand . . .

> MOTHER
> He's back again.
> She starts to lift her hand. Cass stops her.

> CASS
> I'll handle it. I don't want my husband walking around the lobby in pajamas.
> She makes hand motion.

> CASS
> Sorry, darling.

CUT TO:

INT. SITTING ROOM

24 DARRIN   24
whose hand is on the bedroom doorknob, opens door to find himself looking into hotel hallway. In complete bewilderment, he stares back at other door he thought was the hallway door; then, he dazedly goes to bar and picks up champagne glass, and downs it.

CUT TO:

INT. BEDROOM
25   CASS AND MOTHER   25

> MOTHER
> (admiringly)

Very good.

> CASS

I just did that because it's an emergency. I'm through
with that sort of stuff.

> MOTHER
> (shakes head)

What a waste of talent.

> CASS
> (a bit flattered in spite of herself)

True.

> (then quickly)

Mother, you've got to get out of here. Even witchcraft
can't keep him out there all night. It's our honeymoon!

CUT TO:

INT. SITTING ROOM
26   DARRIN   26
still at bar, trying to gird himself for another attempt on the bedroom bastion.

CUT TO:

INT. BEDROOM
27   CASS AND MOTHER   27

> MOTHER

. . .Do you realize the danger you're in? If you live like
one of them for a year . . . without practicing your trade
. . . you *become* one of them.

Establishing conflict and suspense that we may need in future stories.

CASS
Exactly . . . I want nothing more than to be married,
be a good housewife and a helpmate to the man I love.

MOTHER
To think I would ever hear my own daughter say a
thing like that! I'm sending you to a headshrinker.

CASS
I don't need a psychiatrist!

MOTHER
No—no. I mean a real headshrinker!

CUT TO:

INT. SITTING ROOM
28   DARRIN   28
is standing, putting finishing touches on his hair and dressing
gown, preparatory to braving the bedroom once more.

CUT TO:

INT. BEDROOM
29   CASS AND MOTHER   29

MOTHER
I don't know where you get it. It must be from your
father. Certainly not from *my* side of the family.

*I believe this is one of the elements that made this a successful
series. We asked only enough suspension of belief to accept the witchcraft. In most other aspects, we gave them identifiable human feelings and foibles.*

CASS
Mother, he's coming and you're leaving.

MOTHER

Oh, no I'm not!

Cass does her characteristic witch twitch and a traditional witch disappearance gesture toward her mother.

Mother doesn't disappear at all. She stands very much in evidence and smiles.

MOTHER

Me? Matilda? You *are* kidding?

CASS
(embarrassed)

I've never been more serious in my life. Please—?

Mother shakes her head, no. Does a gesture toward the door.

CUT TO:

INT. SITTING ROOM

30   DARRIN   30

is just lifting hand to knock at door.

CUT TO:

INT. LOBBY

31   ANGLE   31

There is Darrin, still in position of knocking at door which isn't there. He looks around confusedly, sheepishly avoids clerk's curious stare and starts once again for stairway.

CLERK

Boy! What a bride he must have!

CUT TO:

This is, of course, what is called a running gag. Very effective, with mounting comedic values, when done properly—which means that each version goes a little farther than the last. Otherwise, it becomes merely repetitious.

INT. BEDROOM

32   CASS AND MOTHER   32

> CASS
>
> Mother, please . . . it's my honeymoon . . . we'd rather be alone.

> MOTHER
>
> I'm not leaving until I know you're all right. You're still young and inexperienced, dear. You don't know the prejudice you'll run into. They think all witches work only one day a year on Halloween . . . And that we still wear those ugly hats and fly around on brooms. What if he finds out you're a witch?

What comedy writers call "laying in" information that will be used later. Especially effective in comedy because it is a straight line both disguised and removed so that it is a surprise when it pays off.

> CASS
>
> I'm going to tell him.

> MOTHER
> (aghast)
>
> You're going to *tell* him!

> CASS
>
> I don't think married people should have secrets from each other.

> MOTHER
>
> When are you going to tell him?

> CASS
>
> Soon as you leave.

> MOTHER
>
> That should solve everything. You'll be back home before you know it.

                         CASS
You're wrong. I think when two people love each oth-
er and have understanding . . .
She looks around. Mother is gone. She sighs with relief.

                         CASS
    Good.
She starts toward door.

                                        CUT TO:

INT. SITTING ROOM
33 DARRIN   33
    is just coming in, still bewildered. Cass opens bedroom door.

                        DARRIN
    The strangest things have been happening. I took one
    glass of champagne and I found myself . . .
His voice trails off as his eyes take in the vision of loveliness
framed in the doorway. All other thoughts are swept from his
mind. She is all his and it's legal. He starts for her.

                         CASS
    Sweetheart . . . let's sit down and talk.

                        DARRIN
    Talk??!!

                                        FLIP TO:

INT. SITTING ROOM
34 DARRIN AND CASS   34

                        DARRIN
    You're a what???!!!

This quick dissolve is a simple device to avoid the worst
kind of exposition. If exposition is deadly, exposition of some-
thing the audience already knows is torturous.

CASS
(quickly)
I'm a witch!

DARRIN
(patronizingly)
That's wonderful. We'll talk about it tomorrow.

CASS
Now! *I am a witch*—a real broom-riding, house-haunt-ing, cauldron-stirring witch.
Darrin thinks this over carefully. He figures it out.

DARRIN
It *must* be the champagne. Now darling, it's been a
hectic day for both of us. This getting married is
tougher than it looks.

CASS
Would I say I am a witch if I'm not?

DARRIN
I don't know. I had an aunt once who thought she was
a lighthouse. She'd always be . . .
(slowly turns head from one side to the other, opening mouth
wide as he does so)

Whenever it rained, she insisted on climbing up on the
garage roof to warn the sailors.

CASS
How do you know she wasn't a lighthouse?

DARRIN
Huh?

CASS
Maybe you were the one who was looking straight at a

lighthouse and thought you were seeing an old lady on a garage roof.

Darrin thinks this over a little and then shakes his head bewilderedly.

>   DARRIN
>   Okay, so my aunt was a lighthouse and you're a
>   witch.
>   (puts his arm around her)
>   Look, honey, we've been married only four hours . . .
>   we can go see a good doctor .. . . *after* our honey-
>   moon.

>   CASS
>   (sadly)
>   You don't believe me.

The obligation of this scene is that Darrin must learn that his wife is a witch. Much of the comedy of the scene comes from the always interesting situation of having the audience privy to information that a character doesn't have.

An example of the principle, as explained by Tennessee Williams: "The audience should know something the character doesn't, the character should know something the audience doesn't, and the writer should make something happen neither of them expects."

>   DARRIN
>   (humoring her)
>   Okay, if you're a witch, where's your black hat and
>   broom? And how come you're out when it isn't even
>   Halloween?

Paying attention? The pay-off on the earlier "laying in."

>   CASS
>   Mother was right . . . You're prejudiced.

>   DARRIN
>   I thought your mother's in India.

CASS

She is, but she dropped in on me this evening.

DARRIN
(going along with the gag)

Here?

(Cass nods.)

DARRIN
(stage whisper)

Is she here now?

CASS

No.

DARRIN

Good. I don't care for even an invisible mother-in-law
on my honeymoon.

CASS

I guess I'll just have to prove to you that I'm a witch.

DARRIN
(indulging her)

That's a good idea. Why don't you prove it?

CASS

I wasn't going to do any more witchcraft . . . for your
sake.

DARRIN

I'll overlook it this time.

CASS

Of course, I'm not very experienced at it.

DARRIN

Well, you're young yet.

CASS
I can do only little things.

DARRIN
A little thing will be fine . . .
(picks up cigarette)
Any old thing.
(tries to light it with table lighter that won't work)
I never yet saw a table lighter that worked . . . Just once I'd
like . . .

She makes hand motion. Miraculously the lighter lights. He
looks at it in surprise for a moment, looks suspiciously at her,
then dismisses the thought.

DARRIN
Look, honey, we all imagine things. I, myself . . .

As he is talking he looks for an ashtray on which to put his cigarette. It's across the table. Before he can reach for it, it moves
under his cigarette. He snatches up his cigarette, stares at the
ashtray for a second and then decides to ignore it.

DARRIN
I, myself, have been imagining . . .

He flicks the ash of his cigarette toward ashtray. It would miss,
except that the ashtray swiftly moves to catch the ash neatly.
This he can't ignore. He picks up ashtray and examines it. He
flicks ash about six inches away from ashtray, which efficiently
moves to catch ashes again. He turns his back on ashtray. Then
suddenly flicks his ashes diametrically opposite to where the
ashtray is. Ashtray swoops around in a ninety-degree semicircle
to catch ashes.

DARRIN
I need some air . . .

He starts for window, but before he can get there, the window
opens.

                    DARRIN
        I wish I had a drink.
A highball appears in his hand.

                    DARRIN
        An old-fashioned.
The highball is replaced by an old-fashioned.

                    DARRIN
        With a cherry on top.
A cherry appears on top of the old-fashioned. He downs drink
in one swallow. Stares at Cass.

                    DARRIN
        You're a witch!

*When is repeating something seven times, as these magic tricks
were, funnier than doing it just six, five, or once, for that matter? Or
why wouldn't the eighth time be even funnier? It might be. There is no
hard and fast rule or even rule-of-thumb answer.*

*What if the Gainsborough Boy had been a darker shade of blue?
Or Rachmaninoff's prelude in D sharp minor? It only serves to
remind us that in any art form, we eventually get to the part which
cannot be taught, measured, proven, or guaranteed—by anybody.
Most of the time, in most of the best things, you must fly without a net.
Otherwise, executives and machines would have all the worthwhile
credits. It is rhythm, timing, or sometimes just feel. But that—with
craft—is your best shot at getting the effective brush stroke, the
pleasing bar of music, or the line that brings the explosive laugh.*

*Note: Those executives and machines can manufacture the sure-
fire laugh—called a laugh track—and it was probably done here. But
it doesn't count—believe it—it doesn't count until we can get, from
the final consumer—a real live person—a real live laugh.*

                    CASS
        That's what I've been trying to tell you.
Darrin, stunned, starts to sit down. He would have ended up on
the floor but a chair quickly moves under him.

                    DARRIN
                    (dully)
Thanks.
Cass crosses to him.

                    CASS
Darling, are you all right?

                    DARRIN
Yes—no—no, I'm not all right. My first marriage and
my first witch all in one day. I don't deserve such hap-
piness.
Cass starts to sit in his lap. He holds up his hand to stop her.

                    DARRIN
Would you mind moving that ashtray again?

                    CASS
Do I have to?

                    DARRIN
                    (firmly)
Yes.
Cass makes the ashtray move.

                    DARRIN
                (complete acceptance)
You're a witch all right.

See, we did do it eight times.

Cass sits in his lap and snuggles.

                    CASS
I suppose I shouldn't have married you but . . . I love
you so much, Darrin.

                    DARRIN
I love you, too, but I hadn't figured on this.

CASS

I'll make you a good wife, Darrin . . . I promise.

DARRIN

This is not something like somebody who just thinks
she's a lighthouse.

*Another running gag. Which not only builds but saves the invest-
ment of a separate straight line.*

CASS

And you've got to take into consideration that I'm not
one of those . . .
(waves arms)
. . . big, important witches who cause typhoons and
things. I'm just a . . .
(moves her hands together to show how small)
. . . little witch.

*This was the subject of much thought and many subsequent
meetings. How much witchcraft can a witch do? To make her more
vulnerable and sympathetic, I decided that she should be a minor
witch with minor powers. It was an issue that provoked many
discussions and arguments. I remember, at one point, defending
some witchcraft which others thought inadmissible. I said, more in
frustration than in arrogance, "She's my witch and she can do
anything I want her to do."*

*There is a famous, and by now classic story told by writers
about a related subject. Years ago, a writer for the popular series,
"My Favorite Martian," was summoned to the oak-paneled office of
a network executive and rebuked for a line of dialogue he had written
for the visitor from another planet. "A Martian," the executive, well-
paid for these insights, chided, "wouldn't say that."*

DARRIN

Maybe we should go see a marriage counselor.
Cass holds him close.

CASS

I love you so much, Darrin.

She snuggles even closer. He's now becoming aware that he has a lovely girl wearing a negligee in his arms and it's getting to him. She kisses him.

DARRIN

We've got to figure this out.

This time he kisses her, long, languorously. Comes up for air.

DARRIN

. . . Later.

Bends her back in passionate kiss, as we PULL BACK through window to reveal a cat moving along the window ledge high above the city. It meows.

FADE FOR:

COMMERCIAL

FADE OUT

One of the very few advantages, if not the only one, of the commercial is that it can be used as the rug under which to sweep "dirty" sex in the straitlaced world of television. We are all aware of how inhibited the medium is, but most are not aware that censorship is much more oppressive in the field of comedy. Which usually makes sex in television comedies leering, teasing, and hypocritical. This is because television—mirroring the most restrictive of Judeo-Christian mores—allows sex only if it's portentous and unenjoyable: conditions which are not very conducive to humor.

The censorship department, itself going by the euphemistic name of "Program Practices," in one of the many of its hypocritical contradictions, will label any kind of physical sex distasteful in a comedy that may advertise an under-arm deodorant or sanitary napkins. In a soap opera, on the other hand, the same program practices department on the same network will allow characters to jump in and out of bed with a variety of partners, including sometimes those of the same family and sometimes even of the same gender.

FADE IN:

INT.BAR—DAY

35   DARRIN   35
    is at bar with his friend, DAVE.

The following scene had two purposes. The first was to establish Darrin's best friend, whom we expected to be a running character. (As was noted before, that didn't happen.)

The second reason is that in the name of integrity, we are following the logical sequence in a story of a man who has found out he married a witch. Integrity and logic in storytelling are as important, if not more important, in comedy, farce, or fantasy. We ask the audience for a suspension of belief—that a boy is from outer space, or a man can become invisible at will, or a woman is a witch—and after they do this for us, we must honor their trust by being logical in every other phase. Also, not to make our motive sound too high-flown, it makes the story more powerful, the comedy more effective.

So in the name of logic, a man who's found he's married a witch will feel the need for support and counsel. However, an important part of the story construction is that no other mortal knows she is a witch. So, as seen in the next three sequences, the devices used are: first, not listening, second, not believing, and third, not taking him seriously.

> DAVE
> And if you can't talk to your best friend, who can you talk to? I know all about marriage . . . That's why I'm a bachelor.

Another favorite target. The second oldest profession must be making fun of marriage.

> DARRIN
> Well, here's my problem, Dave.

> DAVE
> The Sea of Matrimony is beset with hidden shoals and reefs.

DARRIN

I found out that Cassandra is a witch.

DAVE

And it takes Tolerance and Understanding to find the Channel of True Love.

Neither really hears the other as they're both off on their own tangents.

DARRIN

I didn't believe it at first, until she started to move around ashtrays and things.

DAVE

Marriage is a partnership where two people, side by side, face life's obstacles together.

DARRIN

I can't tell my family . . .

DAVE

But when two people love each other, *really* love each other, it will work out.

DARRIN

They got enough trouble getting my aunt off the garage roof whenever it's raining.

Another example of the "running" gag, or "milking" it, if it's gone on too long.

DAVE

Adjustment . . . That's the Foundation on which every lasting marriage is built . . . Adjust.

DARRIN

Of course, there might be certain advantages . . . Like if you want a drink in a dry state.

(Again, a play on something that's been set-up before saves us the use of a straight line.)

                    DAVE
               (consults watch)
    Well, I've got to go.
                    (slaps Darrin on back)
    Look, if you ever need any help or advice again, feel free
    to call me.

                    DARRIN
       Thanks.
                    (sits glumly as Dave exits.)

                                        DISSOLVE TO:

INT. DOCTOR'S OFFICE—DAY
36 DARRIN   36
       is sitting facing Doctor's desk.

                    DARRIN
    Doc, you and I have been friends for a long time. I don't
    know whether you can help, but I just had to bring this
    problem to you.

                    DOCTOR
               (calmly)
    Darrin—that's what I'm here for. Just tell me what's
    bothering you.

                                        DISSOLVE TO:

                    DARRIN
    I'm married to a witch—a real live, house-haunting,
    broom-riding, cauldron-stirring, card-carrying witch.
    There is a pause.

                    DOCTOR
    Very simple problem . . . now that you've had your

honeymoon, you need a vacation.
>(writes prescription)
And take these three times a day.

(The psychiatrist has long ago passed mother-in-law in the sweep-stakes for the favorite comedy butt. This popularity is, I believe, be-cause he is often thought of as aloof, intimidating, and incomprehen-sible, which makes not only fertile ground for humor but cries out for the relief of the put-down laugh that will make him less fearsome.)

INT. BAR—DAY

37   DARRIN   37

is now sitting there alone. He had obviously had a couple of drinks. BARTENDER wordlessly points to Darrin's glass. Dar-rin nods. Bartender refills glass.

>DARRIN
Al . . . My wife is a witch.

>BARTENDER
You should see *my* wife.

DISSOLVE TO:

INT. LIVING ROOM—NIGHT

38   CASS AND DARRIN   38

He is pacing floor. She is sitting quietly in the corner of a couch before the fire, watching his every move, hanging on every word.

>DARRIN
And I've gone over it and over it in my mind and I've come to a decision . . .

He turns to face her. She waits breathlessly.

>DARRIN
I love you and I can't give you up.

She flings herself into his arms happily.

CASS

Oh, darling, darling . . . I'll be the best wife any man ever had.

DARRIN
(holds her off)
Now, wait . . . We're going to live a *normal* life . . .
(sits down)
You're not to . . .
Miraculously the hassock comes under his feet.

DARRIN

Cut that out!

CASS

I'm sorry, dear. I forgot myself.

DARRIN

No more witchcraft. You promise?

Reinforcing the all-important conflict.

CASS

I promise. And, darling, after a while we'll be a normal, happy couple, with no problems . . . just like everybody else.

DARRIN

It's not going to be easy. It's tough enough to be married to an advertising man if you're normal. You'll have to learn to be a suburban housewife.

A little jab at another favorite target—the advertising business. The humorist, like the hunter, looks ceaselessly for a game and, like a good hunter, doesn't shoot at anything too weak or too small.

CASS
(eagerly)
I'll learn . . . you'll see . . . I'll learn.

                    DARRIN
You'll have to learn to cook . . .
Cass nods agreeably.

                    DARRIN
. . .keep house. . .
She nods.

                    DARRIN
Go to my mother's for dinner every Friday night . . .
She nods.

                    DARRIN
Entertain clients . . .
She nods.

                    DARRIN
. . . and spend quiet evenings at home watching TV
and pasting trading stamps into books.

                    CASS
It sounds wonderful, dear, we'll be just like everybody
else . . . And after we're settled, maybe my mother could
come to visit for a . . .
(she trails off as she sees the startled look on his face)
maybe we'd better work up to that gradually. Oh, darling,
I'll try . . . I promise I'll try.
He puts his arms around her fondly.

                    DARRIN
I'm glad that's settled. Let's sit down and have some tea.
She starts to make motion with her hand. Stopped at his glare.

                    CASS
                  (happily)
I'll *make* it all by myself.
Throws a kiss at him and exits. Darrin is lost in thought.

DARRIN
We'll work it out some way . . . So my wife is a
witch . . .
(looks directly into camera)
Every married man has to make *some* adjustments.

SLOW FADE

MIDDLE BREAK

*This is the middle break. Although I feel we've been economical
and efficient in the use of our time, this demonstrates a problem pe-
culiar to the pilot episode. We've taken eleven minutes, almost half of
the allotted twenty-four and a half (the time remaining after subtrac-
tion of commercials, station identification, billboard, etc. from a
thirty-minute show) to establish the characters, setting, and general
premise for the series.* We haven't even started the plot. *In the subsequent episodes, of this or any other half-hour series, the story will be
started well within the first few minutes—perhaps the first thirty seconds.*

*So, we have about thirteen minutes left to give the audience what
they came for—a story. A complete, three-act beginning, middle and
end story. Not an easy task, nor conducive to the best writing, but
necessary for the opening episode of a new series. And a challenge—
but unlike the triple somersault from the flying trapeze—the professional tries to make it look easy.*

FADE IN:
INT. KITCHEN—DAY

| 39 | CLOSE SHOT—SINK | 39 |

full of dirty dishes.

. . . and how's that for identification.

CUT TO:

| 40 | CLOSE SHOT | 40 |

Disordered array of ingredients for cake.

CUT TO

| 41 | CLOSE SHOT | 41 |

Two opened eggs on plate, behind which is a book propped

open at page reading:

"Angel Food Cake"

Separate the yolks from the whites of two eggs . . ."
We see a spoon come into shot trying to separate the white from
the yolk, unsuccessfully, of course, because the white keeps
oozing back. Then the spoon tries to pick up the yolk. It breaks,
mixing with the white. CAMERA PULLS BACK to reveal
Cass in a very disordered kitchen. Her hair is disheveled, her
demeanor rather desperate. She puts the eggs into the mixture
under mixer and turns the switch. The entire concoction whirls
around, spraying her and the room. Cass gives up.

CASS
(wails)

Mother!

After the children go to bed, and outside of news and sports events,
women are the chief manipulator of the dial. So we get brownie
points for showing that even someone with supernatural powers has
trouble doing a housewife's job.

Mother appears. She peers into bowl.

MOTHER

That's an interesting brew. What does it do?

CASS

I was trying to bake a cake. Mother, I don't know how
I'm going to manage. I've got to do the dishes, clean
    the kitchen, vacuum and dust, make the beds, shop,
and then prepare dinner.

MOTHER

Tsk . . . tsk . . . How did a nice witch like you ever
get into a spot like this?
Phone rings. Mother squeals in surprise.

MOTHER

What's that?

CASS
(wearily)
The phone again. It's been ringing all morning with
people trying to sell me encyclopedias and roofing for
the house.

Obviously the operative word here is identification. Not indispensa-
ble but always a dependable tool. As you will see in the subsequent
incidents, we use the juxtaposition of the mysterious other-world
against the prosaic, everyday routine with which we are all familiar,
for comedic values.

MOTHER
(eagerly)
Can I answer it?

CASS
Go ahead.
Cass starts to put dishes in sink while Mother picks up phone.

MOTHER
(in phone)
Hello?
(to Cass)
Somebody wants to know when the Revolutionary War
was fought.

CASS
Oh, Mother . . .!
(takes phone from Mother and speaks into it.)
I beg your pardon?
(hands phone back to Mother in surprise)
You're right.

MOTHER
(in phone)
Which Revolutionary War were you referring to, honey?
I've seen them all . . . Oh, that one . . . Let's see . . . that's
when Salem was *the* place to live . . . Oh, yes . . . That was

in 1776 . . . Of course I'm right, I was there . . . Oh, isn't
that sweet . . .
>(to Cass)

He says I just won four free Bossa Nova lessons . . .
>(in phone)

That's very kind of you, honey, and since you're so sweet,
I'll teach you a dance in exchange . . . We've got to wait
for a full moon . . . and then if you get a cauldron and grind
up some bats and—
>(to Cass)

He hung up.

Cass meanwhile has finished stacking dishes in dishwasher.
Only she simply stacks them instead of putting them in the
racks.

MOTHER

What's that?

CASS

It washes dishes.

MOTHER

Imagine! Do you know the right words?

CASS
>(reading directions)

You don't use words . . . You just press this button.

She presses the button and through glass door we can see the jets
of water and agitator smashing dishes to smithereens.

MOTHER

Unbelievable . . . And a great improvement over those
complicated incantations.

CASS

Mother, if you could help me instead of . . .

MOTHER

Okay, okay . . .

She walks out of shot. Cass, in cleaning up, notices electric can opener. She studies it, puts a can in, presses button and then looks at opened can, awed.

> CASS
>
> What do you know!

She turns to mother. But Mother isn't there. Concerned, Cass goes into living room looking for her.

INT. LIVING ROOM

42   ANGLE   42

Mother is serenely resting on couch thumbing through Science Fiction magazine while the vacuum cleaner is working by itself, and a dustcloth, untouched by human hands, is dusting.

> CASS
>
> Mother, stop that.

With a wave of her hand, Mother does.

> MOTHER
>
> You wanted me to help.

> CASS
>
> I told you. I intend to be a good wife and housekeeper without ever again resorting to witchcraft.

> MOTHER
>
> Offhand, I'd say that's impossible.

Sound of doorbell.

> CASS
>
> Somebody's at the door.
> (starts to go, stops)
> Mother, you'd better keep out of sight.

> MOTHER
>
> Okay, okay.
> (starts to go, then turns back to get magazine)
> I'm in the middle of a story on how a mad doctor has

invented a potion to make himself disappear.

She leaves with magazine. Cass crosses to door and opens it. There stand two women, ELSIE and JUNE, in housedresses. They are attractive, young housewives of about Cass's apparent age. One of them carries a cake.

> ELSIE

How do you do.

> CASS

How do you do.

> ELSIE

I'm Elsie Hopkins and this is June Bergstrom. We're your neighbors and we thought we'd welcome you into the neighborhood.

> CASS

Thank you, I'm Cass Stevens.

> JUNE

We brought this cake . . . as a sort of housewarming gift.

> CASS

That's very sweet. Won't you come in?

At these words an eight-year-old boy, ROBERT, unseen up until now, squeezes in between the women and darts into living room.

> ELSIE

That's my boy, Robert.
> (calls)

Now, Robert, you behave.

> CASS

Oh, he looks nice, I . . .

Another boy, about six, squeezes through and darts after Robert.

ELSIE
That's June's boy. We each have one.

CASS
Isn't that . . .

Another boy, about four, darts between them and into room.
Cass looks at him in surprise.

ELSIE
I don't know who he is.

JUNE
Now, children, if you want to stay here, you'll have to
sit quiet.

CASS
Oh, that's all right. I don't mind.

The boys take this as permission to move around at will, examining everything. The women sit down.

ELSIE
We'd also like to invite you to join our Tuesday Culture Club.

CASS
Thank you.

By this time the boys have disappeared out of the shot.

JUNE
We meet every Tuesday afternoon and discuss current
events.

ELSIE
Then we have cookies and lemonade and play Lotto
for a bottle of cologne provided by the hostess.

CUT TO:

Demonstrates that which, a very short time ago, was the male ver-

sion of what a housewife does while he's out making a living. Sexist, of course. We wouldn't do it today and would probably get our heads knocked off if we tried.

INT. BEDROOM
43   ANGLE   43
   Mother is stretched out on bed reading the magazine. The three
   boys file into room and stare at her.

> ROBERT
Hi.

> MOTHER
Hi . . . Who are you?

> ROBERT
I'm Black Bob, the fastest gun in the West.

> STEPHEN
I'm an Indian . . .
>   (makes Indian sound with hand over mouth)
> And he's . . .
>   (indicates smallest boy)
> . . . a horse.

> ROBERT
Who are you?

> MOTHER
I'm a witch.

> ROBERT
>   (matter of fact)
> Okay.

A child's disarming credibility, and willing suspension of belief is not only charming but excellent fuel for comedy.

> STEPHEN
You a good witch or a bad witch?

MOTHER

Comme ci, comme ça.

ROBERT
(shouts)

Here come the bad guys!

Stephen darts behind a chair and starts shooting. Robert hastily crawls over bed to get out of range. The little one paws the ground. Mother draws her legs up to get them out of the way.

MOTHER

Now, here, be careful.

CUT TO:

INT. LIVING ROOM

44   ANGLE   44

ELSIE

. . . And they pick up the trash every Tuesday.

JUNE

But you've got to remember to keep the papers and cans separate.

Cass is looking from one to the other bewilderedly, trying to keep it straight.

ELSIE

They pick up the cans on the first Tuesday of every month.

JUNE

Unless there are five Tuesdays in a month.

ELSIE

Then they pick them up on the last Thursday of the preceding month.

CUT TO:

INT. BEDROOM

45 ANGLE   45

It is in shambles. All three are behind overturned chairs, holding lamps for protection, shooting at each other.

> MOTHER
>
> Now, boys, be careful.

> ROBERT
>
> Get her. She's a bad guy!

They advance upon her.

CUT TO:

INT. LIVING ROOM

46 ANGLE   46

> ELSIE
>
> . . . And of course, we don't want the street widened . . . You know, all that traffic coming through. So Monday, we're going to picket the bulldozers.

> JUNE
>
> We're forming teams of two girls each to take turns picketing.

> ELSIE
>
> There's an opening on the refreshment committee to serve coffee and doughnuts to the pickets.

> JUNE
> (listening)
> Those boys are awfully quiet.

> CASS
>
> Yes, isn't that nice.

> ELSIE
>
> Boys are always dangerous when quiet.

Both girls start toward bedroom. Cass tries to head them off but they don't even notice.

CUT TO:

INT. BEDROOM

47   ANGLE   47

All three boys are neatly and harmlessly tied and gagged. Elsie, June, and Cass come in. Elsie unties Robert's gag.

Mischievous boys, another great target. Notice how much fun there is getting even?

> ELSIE
>
> What are you boys up to?

> ROBERT
>
> There was a witch in here and she tied and gagged us.

> ELSIE
> (matter of fact)
>
> Okay . . . okay.
> (to June, who is untying the others)
> We'd better get them home.

> JUNE
> (to Cass)
>
> They are so . . .
> (stops, suddenly puzzled)
> How did all *three* get tied up?

Elsie is also puzzled for a second. Then shrugs.

> ELSIE
> (explaining)
>
> Boys . . .

The women exit, herding the boys in front of them. Cass follows, but turns to take one look around the room first. Where's Mother? She looks up.

48

MOTHER—CASS'S POV   48

She is comfortably reclined above wardrobe reading the magazine.

MOTHER
The mad doctor has an invention that counteracts the law
of gravity . . . And they're chasing him across a ceiling . . .
So he opens a skylight and they all fall up.

CASS
Mother, we've got work to do.

MOTHER
(climbing down)
Where do those writers *get* those cockamamie ideas?

DISSOLVE TO:

INT. DARRIN'S OUTER OFFICE
49   ANGLE ON DOOR   49
        reading:
"McMANN AND TATE, ADVERTISING, Darrin Stevens,
vice-pres."
Sheila comes into shot and opens door.

*I did not write the following scene. In a letter to me (I was on an-
other assignment at the time), the executive producer explained ". . .
We felt that Sheila needed a little more dimension and that her prior
relationship with Darrin needed to be underscored . . . Please do not
feel that anyone has been rewriting your material because they felt it
necessary to do so . . . These changes were made in the interest of
time . . ." Revision of a script by nonwriters is common. Explaining
and apologizing to the writer is rare. I can only guess that it was because I had the reputation of being a "sensitive" writer, and nobody
wanted an upset writer around to rock the boat. Or maybe I'm being
cynical. It might have been simply a courteous gesture by nice people. That's also possible.
    A reputation for being sensitive is a dangerous deterrent to the
employability of a writer. However, at this stage in my career, when I
found it made them careful of making arbitrary script changes, I not
only didn't deny the reputation, I encouraged it.
    I felt the information in this added scene was done briefly and*

adequately in a phone call you will read later. Admittedly, phone calls are not recommended for comedy or drama, but I decided this was the lesser of two evils. It was felt by the others, however, that the character of Sheila was so important in this story that this exposition scene was necessary. I didn't agree, but there were two undeniable facts. I couldn't prevent it and anyway, I was presumed to be prejudiced about my script. Two more undeniable facts: one, a writer is always prejudiced about his own work, and two, that does not necessarily mean he's wrong.

CUT TO:

INT. DARRIN'S OFFICE
50   ANGLE   50
Sheila enters. Darrin scrambles to his feet.

SHEILA
Darrin!

DARRIN
(not too sure of the reception he will receive)
Sheila!
He laughs nervously, tries to pretend nothing is wrong, offers his hand stiffly. She ignores it and plants a kiss on his mouth.

SHEILA
Darling, I just got back from Nassau yesterday. I've been trying to reach you. I left a message with your secretary. When I didn't hear from you, I decided to invade your office. Why didn't you call me?

DARRIN
Well, Sheila . . . uh . . . You see . . . I just got back from . . . Actually I . . . well . . . I was . . . I mean I am . . . That's some tan you've got there.

SHEILA
Thank you, sweetheart. But why didn't you . . .

DARRIN
(takes a deep breath and plunges)

I'm married!

SHEILA
I know, dearest! Congratulations.

DARRIN
(numb)
Thank you. but how . . .?
(she's smiling)
Don't you care?

SHEILA
(warmly)
Oh, sweetheart. Care? Of course I care. After all, if I hadn't left for Nassau when I did, it might have been me. But no hard feelings, you sneak. I couldn't be happier for you. I'm sure she's an angel.

SHEILA
Darling, I called to ask the two of you to drop over tonight if you hadn't any other plans. A few of the gang are coming over for potluck. I realize it's rather short notice . . . nothing fancy . . . very relaxed. Sitting-on-the-floor kind of stuff.

DARRIN
Well, that's very nice of you, Sheila. But I don't know.

SHEILA
Darrin, I don't understand.

DARRIN
Well . . . it's just that it might be too soon to spring a whole new set of people on her. She's not quite used to . . .

SHEILA
Too soon!? Don't be silly. Darrin, we're your friends. We are dying to meet her. I simply won't take no for an answer. Seven-thirty tonight. I've got to dash. See you later.

Sheila leaves and he is happy.

DISSOLVE TO:

The scene is harmless, you say? True. But you don't win awards by doing harmless scenes. It took precious screen time off a script from which we had to cut more entertaining, if not more necessary, lines. An example of why a writer will often complain about a scene that looks all right to others. Only he knows how much better it might have been.

INT. KITCHEN—DAY
51   CLOSE SHOT—OPEN DISHWASHER   51

> MOTHER'S VOICE
> They're clean, all right. Now how do you get them back together again?

CAMERA PULLS BACK, REVEALS Mother and Cass staring in dishwasher, the latter very sadly. The kitchen is a mess. Cass starts to sob.

> CASS
> Everything's going wrong. I'll never learn.

Buries her head on Mother's shoulder.

> MOTHER
> (sympathetically)
> Dishwashers . . . women's clubs . . . freeways . . . I'd be frightened to death, too. This normal world is crazy.

Sound: Phone rings.

> MOTHER
> (starts for phone)
> That must be that nice man who wants to teach me the Bossa Nova . . .

> CASS
> (stops her)

I'd better get it . . .
Cass crosses to phone.

It is amazing to me that, in rereading this script, carefully written and performed years ago, I find so many changes I would like to make. This stage cross, like most crosses to the phone, front door, etc. are dead stage waits. If they can't be avoided, they should be covered by a plot line or joke. Perhaps (this was) done on the sound stage. A competent director will usually correct it, if necessary. But unless a director also happens to be a good writer, it will be only coincidental and you can't bank on it. So you had best write the line yourself.

CASS
(on phone)

Hello . . .

MOTHER

Ask him if I can bring a friend.

At least I covered the stage wait there.

Cass puts hand over mouthpiece.

CASS

It's my husband . . .
(happily)
I won't have to make dinner tonight!
During following phone conversation, Mother wanders over to electric waxer. Curiously handles it. It turns on as she accidentally touches button. She jumps away but the waxer keeps following her. She tries to reach over and turn it off but it keeps attacking. In desperation, she makes magical move with her hand and waxer stops. She makes another move of her hand and it retires to corner. One more angry move and it obediently lies down. Mother gives the defeated waxer a triumphant "that'll show you" look.

And there.

CUT TO:

INT. DARRINS OFFICE

52   DARRIN, ON PHONE   52

                       DARRIN

. . . And she asked us to drop over for a potluck supper
with a few of my old chums . . . I don't think you've met
her. I happened to run into her today . . . No. She says
wear something casual . . . It's just a sort of last minute
thing . . . Hmm? Oh, she's just an old friend.

*Seems as though I'm violating my own previously stated rules,
doesn't it? Repeating exposition that the audience already knows.
Actually these were the original lines that were to serve the function
that the added office scene between Darrin and Sheila repeated.
When the newer scene was added, these now repetitive lines of
exposition should have been eliminated. One reason why writers cry
a lot.*

CUT TO:

INT. KITCHEN

53   CASS, ON PHONE   53

                       CASS

How old?

                 DARRIN'S VOICE

Well, I don't know—she's just a friend.

                       CASS

What do you mean by "just a friend"?

                 DARRIN'S VOICE

Well, Sheila and I were . . . were . . . *friends.*

                       CASS

You mean like you went fishing with her and played poker
with her and . . .

> DARRIN'S VOICE
> (laughs)
> No . . . not Sheila. Sheila's more the indoor type.

> CASS
> What!

> DARRIN'S VOICE
> (hastily)
> Darling, it's . . . well, nothing. Don't worry, you'll enjoy
> yourself tonight.

> CASS
> All right, dear. I'll be ready. Goodbye.
> (hangs up phone happily)
> It's all solved. We're going out to dinner tonight. *See . . . I
> didn't need witchcraft.*

> MOTHER
> I don't know what you've got against witchcraft. Any
> woman would love to be a witch . . . Else, why do so many
> of them try so hard?

> DISSOLVE TO:

*Only the standard sit-com husband wouldn't know a siren when
he sees one and realize that she's up to no good.*

*End of first act. We've got the setting, the personae, and the
problem.*

EXT. SHEILA'S HOME—NIGHT
54 FULL SHOT 54
Car drives up. It's rather an imposing-looking house. Darrin
and Cass get out and approach door. Cass is dressed in simple
skirt and blouse with hair tied in back, and flats.

> CASS
> (dubiously)
> It is a pretty fancy-looking house. You think I should
> have dressed more . . .

DARRIN
(interrupts)
It's just a little get-together. She particularly said you
should dress casually.
(starts to press doorbell; stops)
Now Cass, I want you to promise . . . No tricks.

CASS
Darling, I told you I'm not . . .

DARRIN
Promise.

CASS
Scout's honor.
She raises her right hand with fingers crossed.

DARRIN
Not that way.
He uncrosses her fingers and puts the thumb and little finger in
scout's salute. He presses doorbell.

DARRIN
This will be a good opportunity to start learning to fit
into a normal life . . . a casual little get-together . . .
Door is opened by butler who stands aside. Cass is transfixed
with hand still held up in scout salute, until Darrin nudges her
and they enter foyer.

INT. ENTRY HALL—NIGHT
55   CASS AND DARRIN   55
They stop dead as they see drawing room of impeccably dressed
guests having cocktails.

56

ANGLE ON SHEILA   56
as she comes forward to greet them. She is beautifully dressed,

perfectly coiffured, assured . . . the type any woman can hate.

SHEILA

Darrin, *Darling*.

She throws her arms around Darrin and gives him a very warm
kiss. Cass watches. This is a little too affectionate for the casual
friendship Darrin described.

SHEILA

And this is your little bride?
She takes Cass's hand.

CASS

How do you do.

SHEILA

Oh, Darrin . . . she's *sweet*.

*Starting slowly, with a little patronizing, to get the audience to
hate her.*

CASS
(uncomfortably)
I guess I should have dressed more . . .

SHEILA

Not at all, dear. You look . . . sweet. I can tell you're the
type that always dresses so . . . so . . . so *sensibly* . . . You
know—the capable type. Darrin, I'll bet she's good at
typing, cooking, and taking care of the household ac-
counts and playing golf and all those things poor little me
can't do at all.

Cass opens her mouth to answer but Sheila continues.

SHEILA

Won't you come in and meet my friends?
She precedes them into living room. Darrin speaks through the
side of his mouth to Cass.

DARRIN
Sweetheart, I think you're being jobbed. Want to get a
sudden headache and leave?

*Proves he's a nice guy and wants to protect his wife. Another un-
breakable rule on television series comedy. The leads may be stupid,
narrow-minded, or even homely, but they must be likeable. Even Archie Bunker loved his daughter and wife. If you don't care about
them, you won't care about their problems.*

CASS
(through clenched teeth)
I will not.
She forces a smile as she walks into the living room.

SHEILA
Folks, I want you to meet Darrin's little bride.
They all, including Darrin, turn toward Cass who tries to make
a brave little smile but would much rather disappear through the
floor.

DISSOLVE TO:

*End of second act. Even in comedy, perhaps especially in comedy, the
three-act construction is important. Although the acts, as in this example, are rarely proportionate.*

INT. DINING ROOM—NIGHT
57   GROUP SHOT   57
They are all around table. Darrin is sitting on Sheila's right and
she has him monopolized in intimate conversation. Cass is at
the foot of the table next to a portly, middle-aged man more interested in his food than anything else. Cass looks uncomfortably lonely.

DARRIN
Are you all right, dear?

CASS

Fine, fine . . . thank you.

SHEILA

Now don't worry about Cassandra. Since she's a stranger, we're going to help her. Now first dear, we'll have to get you a *good* dressmaker.

CASS

But I don't need . . .

SHEILA

And then we'll introduce you to Pierre. He does wonders with hard-to-manage hair . . . Incidentally, we must have met somewhere before . . . Newport?

Cass shakes her head.

SHEILA

The Riviera?
(sudden idea) The Debutantes' Ball! When did you come out?

CASS

Three weeks ago.

All look at her in amazement.

DARRIN
(hastily)
She means she came out of *New York* three weeks ago. She's been traveling with her parents.

SHEILA

Talking about traveling . . . do you remember the time, Darrin, we ran into each other in Paris and you
. . .

She whispers something obviously wickedly amusing in Darrin's ear. Cass angrily starts making gesture with her hand and a plate of soup starts to slide toward Sheila.

This was before we know that Liz had that delightful nose twitch in her repertoire.

Cass thinks better of it, stops in midmotion, and soup plate stops sliding. Cass turns to see if her dinner companion has noticed.

                         MAN
Good soup.

                         CASS
Yes, it is.

                         MAN
     Sheila always looks so beautiful. Never a hair out of place.
Cass looks up to notice Sheila staring at her. Cass gets self-conscious. She fumbles with her dress and her hair. Is something wrong?

                        SHEILA
Do you know Dr. Hafter, dear?

                         CASS
I beg your pardon?

                        SHEILA
 Dr. Hafter . . . the plastic surgeon . . . does beautiful nose work.

                         CASS
I don't know him.

                        SHEILA
Funny . . . I could have sworn . . . Oh, well . . .

Building to the showdown. Making the villain so hateful that the audience is itching to see her get her comeuppance. Chaplin was, of course, master at this. The villain was always big, always rich, always arrogant, and when the dislike for him peaked, then and only then would he get the pie in the face and fall into the mud puddle, and the audience would explode with gratified laughter.

She goes back to talking to Darrin.

58   CLOSE SHOT—CASS'S FISTS   58
clenched tightly in lap.

Not yet, Cassandra. Tease them a little more.

> CASS
> (half to herself)
> I won't do it . . . I promised Darrin . . . I won't do it
> . . . I won't do it.

> MAN
> You won't do what?

> CASS
> I won't . . .

Her attention is caught by Sheila who has leaned over and is intimately whispering in Darrin's ear while her hand covers his.

Now!

> CASS
> Maybe I will . . .

Her hand in her lap makes required motion.

59   SHEILA AND DARRIN   59
She is leaning in to him with an inviting and provocative smile when a lock of hair drops over her face. She irritatedly pushes it back, pins it, and starts to lean in again.

60   CASS   60
She makes a motion.

61   SHEILA   61
as she leans in, the plate of soup moves just enough so that her

elbow gets in it. She wipes off elbow with her napkin, covers her irritation, starts to lean forward to him again, when the same lock of hair comes down. As she starts to put it back, a shoulder strap slips. She is now busy with the shoulder strap and hair when she looks down.

> SHEILA

My zipper!

The MAID, holding platter, tries to help. A plate of cooked vegetables slides onto Sheila's lap.

> SHEILA
> (shrieks)

What *are* you doing!

> MAID
> (bewildered)

I don't know. I thought I was carrying an empty tray.

Darrin glances suspiciously at Cass, who smiles innocently. Sheila, holding hair with one hand and zipper with the other, starts to hurry out. Her heel catches in the rug and breaks off.

> SHEILA

My heel!

She is now a real mess as she bounces out on one heel, holding zipper with one hand and hair with the other.

Gratification is an important element of humor, and knowing that this rich, conceited snob looks ridiculous, gives us lots.

Darrin is looking at Sheila's plight pityingly. Just then her bracelet falls to floor and Darrin scrambles for it. Sheila is fighting a losing battle for her dignity.

> SHEILA

Of all the idiotic . . .

And let's make sure he'll never like her again.

CUT TO:

62 CASS   62
makes motion.

CUT TO:

63 SHEILA   63
She gets an invisible kick in the derriere.

SHEILA

Ouch!
When she sees nobody within kicking distance, she loses all control, wails, and dashes out.

CUT TO:

64 CASS   64
She is sympathetically batting her innocent eyes.

CASS
(to man)

The soup *is* wonderful . . . I'll just *have* to get the recipe.

FADE FOR:

COMMERCIAL

FADE OUT

The following is the tag. Usually just a joke so that the announcer can say, ". . . Cass and Darrin will be back in a moment" . . . and hold you through the commercial.

FADE IN:
INT. KITCHEN—NIGHT
65 ANGLE   65
Cass is there looking around disconcertedly. It is in the same mess she left it and she doesn't know where to start. Darrin comes in wearing dressing gown. From behind he puts his arms around her waist.

> DARRIN
>
> I'm sorry things went wrong at Sheila's and she got a
> little hysterical—
> > (he stops suddenly)
>
> Say, you didn't have anything to do with—

It always helps in sit-coms if the husband is slightly retarded.

> CASS
>
> Me? What could I—

> DARRIN
>
> Okay . . . okay. Honey, you looked wonderful, and you
> made a big hit with everyone.

> CASS
>
> Thank you, darling.

> DARRIN
>
> You see, if you just go along, things will work out
> *normally.* You don't need any of that . . .
> > (makes motion with his hand)

> CASS
>
> I'm never going to do it again. I promised.

*Otherwise it would cut down dreadfully on both future conflicts
and story premises.*

> DARRIN
>
> That's my girl . . .
> > (nuzzles her frequently)
>
> Why don't we get out of this kitchen?

> CASS
>
> I've just *got* to get it straightened up first.

*In Denmark they did not understand this part. Danes take it for
granted, they patiently explained to me, that a husband would share*

in the kitchen responsibilities. They may have been behind us in comedy, but they were way ahead in women's lib.

> DARRIN
> (whispers into her hair)

Hurry.

I suppose I should know why it is funny to watch a sexually aroused man. I don't.

He exits. Cass determinedly makes start at dishes. The first one slips out of her hand. She gives up.

> CASS

Oh, well . . .

She makes the motion with her hand. Kitchen is immediately cleaned up, with dishes stacked and everything in its place.

> CASS

Maybe I can taper off.

> DARRIN'S VOICE

Sweetheart . . .

> CASS

Coming, darling.

FADE OUT

THE END

Index

Other Books of Interest

General Writing Books

Beginning Writer's Answer Book, edited by Polking and Bloss $14.95
Getting the Words Right: How to Revise, Edit and Rewrite, by Theodore A. Rees Cheney $13.95
How to Become a Bestselling Author, by Stan Corwin $14.95
How to Get Started in Writing, by Peggy Teeters $10.95
How to Write a Book Proposal, by Michael Larsen $9.95
If I Can Write, You Can Write, by Charlie Shedd $12.95
International Writers' & Artists' Yearbook (paper) $12.95
Law & the Writer, edited by Polking & Meranus (paper) $10.95
Knowing Where to Look: The Ultimate Guide to Research, by Lois Horowitz $16.95
Make Every Word Count, by Gary Provost (paper) $7.95
The 29 Most Common Writing Mistakes & How to Avoid Them, by Judy Delton $9.95
Writer's Block & How to Use It, by Victoria Nelson $12.95
Writer's Encyclopedia, edited by Kirk Polking $19.95
Writer's Market, edited by Paula Deimling $19.95
Writer's Resource Guide, edited by Bernadine Clark $16.95
Writing for the Joy of It, by Leonard Knott $11.95
Writing From the Inside Out, by Charlotte Edwards (paper) $9.95

Magazine/News Writing

Complete Guide to Writing Nonfiction, by the American Society of Journalists & Authors $24.95
The Craft of Interviewing, by John Brady $9.95
How to Write & Sell the 8 Easiest Article Types, by Helene Schellenberg Barnhart $14.95
Magazine Writing Today, by Jerome E. Kelley $10.95
Newsthinking: The Secret of Great Newswriting, by Bob Baker $11.95
Stalking the Feature Story, by William Ruehlmann $9.95
Write On Target, by Connie Emerson $12.95

Fiction Writing

Creating Short Fiction, by Damon Knight (paper) $8.95
Fiction Is Folks: How to Create Unforgettable Characters, by Robert Newton Peck $11.95
Fiction Writer's Help Book, by Maxine Rock $12.95
Fiction Writer's Market, edited by Jean Fredette $17.95
Handbook of Short Story Writing, by Dickson and Smythe (paper) $7.95
How to Write Best-Selling Fiction, by Dean R. Koontz $13.95
How to Write Short Stories that Sell, by Louise Boggess (paper) $7.95
One Way to Write Your Novel, by Dick Perry (paper) $6.95
Secrets of Successful Fiction, by Robert Newton Peck $8.95
Storycrafting, by Paul Darcy Boles $14.95
Writing Romance Fiction—For Love And Money, by Helene Schellenberg Barnhart $14.95
Writing the Novel: From Plot to Print, by Lawrence Block (paper) $8.95

Special Interest Writing Books

The Children's Picture Book: How to Write It, How to Sell It, by Ellen E. M. Roberts $17.95
Complete Book of Scriptwriting, by J. Michael Straczynski $14.95
Complete Guide to Writing Software User Manuals, by Brad McGehee (paper) $14.95

Confession Writer's Handbook, by Florence K. Palmer $9.95
The Craft of Lyric Writing, by Sheila Davis $17.95
Guide to Greeting Card Writing, edited by Larry Sandman (paper) $7.95
How to Write a Cookbook and Get It Published, by Sara Pitzer $15.95
How to Write a Play, by Raymond Hull $13.95
How to Write and Sell Your Personal Experiences, by Lois Duncan $10.95
How to Write and Sell (Your Sense of) Humor, by Gene Perret $12.95
How to Write "How-To" Books and Articles, by Raymond Hull (paper) $8.95
How to Write the Story of Your Life, by Frank P. Thomas $12.95
Mystery Writer's Handbook, by The Mystery Writers of America (paper) $8.95
On Being a Poet, by Judson Jerome $14.95
Poet's Handbook, by Judson Jerome $11.95
Programmer's Market, edited by Brad McGehee (paper) $16.95
Sell Copy, by Webster Kuswa $11.95
Successful Outdoor Writing, by Jack Samson $11.95
Travel Writer's Handbook, by Louise Zobel (paper) $9.95
TV Scriptwriter's Handbook, by Alfred Brenner (paper) $9.95
Writing and Selling Science Fiction, by Science Fiction Writers of America (paper) $7.95
Writing for Children & Teenagers, by Lee Wyndham (paper) $9.95
Writing for Regional Publications, by Brian Vachon $11.95
Writing for the Soaps, by Jean Rouverol $14.95
Writing to Inspire, by Gentz, Roddy, et al $14.95

The Writing Business

Complete Guide to Self-Publishing, by Tom & Marilyn Ross $19.95
Complete Handbook for Freelance Writers, by Kay Cassill $14.95
Freelance Jobs for Writers, edited by Kirk Polking (paper) $7.95
How to Be a Successful Housewife/Writer, by Elaine Fantle Shimberg $10.95
How You Can Make $20,000 a Year Writing, by Nancy Hanson (paper) $6.95
The Writer's Survival Guide: How to Cope with Rejection, Success and 99 Other Hang-Ups of the Writing Life, by Jean and Veryl Rosenbaum $12.95

To order directly from the publisher, include $2.00 postage and handling for 1 book and 50¢ for each additional book. Allow 30 days for delivery.

Writer's Digest Books, Department B
9933 Alliance Road, Cincinnati OH 45242
Prices subject to change without notice.